Blueprint for School System Transformation

A Vision for Comprehensive Reform in Milwaukee and Beyond

Edited by Frederick M. Hess and Carolyn Sattin-Bajaj

ROWMAN & LITTLEFIELD EDUCATION
A division of
ROWMAN & LITTLEFIELD
Lanham • New York • Toronto • Plymouth, UK

Published by Rowman & Littlefield Education
A division of Rowman & Littlefield
4501 Forbes Boulevard, Suite 200, Lanham, Maryland 20706
www.rowman.com

10 Thornbury Road, Plymouth PL6 7PP, United Kingdom

Copyright © 2013 by Frederick M. Hess and Carolyn Sattin-Bajaj

British Library Cataloguing in Publication Information Available

Library of Congress Cataloging-in-Publication Data Available

978-1-4758-0468-3 (cloth : alk. paper)—978-1-4758-0469-0 (pbk. : alk. paper)—
ISBN 978-1-4758-0470-6 (electronic)

Printed in the United States of America

Contents

Acknowledgments

This volume is the product of the hard work and devotion of everyone involved. We thank our authors who researched, revised, and discussed their topics without ever wavering in their engagement with the project.

We'd like to offer our heartfelt thanks to the marvelously talented Taryn Hochleitner for her inspiring work ethic and deft editorial touch. Without Taryn's firm supervision and impressive talents, this project would not have enjoyed a fraction of the success it did.

We are immensely grateful for the partnership of the Wisconsin Policy Research Institute and its president George Lightbourn for initiating this project and helping to make it a reality. Thanks are also due to WPRI staff, including Mike Ford and Mike Nichols in particular, for their vital assistance in managing the production of these pieces.

We are ever indebted to the steadfast support provided by AEI and its president, Arthur Brooks, for the support, time, and resources that enable us to address some of the thorniest challenges in education. We are also grateful for the helpful guidance of AEI's vice president Henry Olsen, who provided incisive feedback on this work. We would also like to thank the terrific research staff at AEI for their hard work coordinating the research and editing the contributions. Specifically, we want to thank Lauren Aronson, Daniel Lautzenheiser, Michael McShane, and Jenna Talbot.

Finally, we express our gratitude to the Rowman & Littlefield team, in particular vice president and editorial director Tom Koerner for his skillful direction throughout the course of the project.

Foreword

For twenty years before Katrina, the school district in New Orleans was one of the most tragically dysfunctional and corrupt in the country. School board aspirants ran for office promising waves of "fixing" a "broken system." Fail! Then "good deed doers" elected a slate of reform-minded school board members time and again. Fail! Efforts focused on bringing in the Superman superintendent. Surely, the "Super Super" could do the trick. Fail! Another effort was to focus on the grassroots. Create a diverse group representing races, class, and culture and press for reform. Fail! In the summer of 2005, the academically bottom-of-the-barrel school district was placed in financial receivership of the state, and corrupt officials were being prosecuted and going to jail. Then, to paraphrase Randy Newman's song, Katrina tried to wash us away.

Six years after Hurricane Katrina's floodwaters drained out of the city, there is proof that it was not an ill wind. There is real reason to be hopeful for the children of New Orleans and its education system. Whether it's the 80 percent of schools taken over by the state's Recovery School District (RSD) or the remaining "best schools" left in the hands of the somewhat-traditional Orleans Parish School Board (OPSB), there has been real and significant improvement in all aspects of public education, most importantly academic achievement and high school completion. In fact in the five years since school resumed, based on the state's standards tests, the RSD has doubled the number of students performing at grade level compared to numbers before the storm (from 24 percent to 51 percent passing). The students attending school board schools have done well also. The four-year cohort graduation rate for all students in New Orleans (RSD and OPSB) has catapulted to 78 percent, higher than the state average and higher than any of the large urban districts in Louisiana. That the city of New Orleans schools and students could do so well was unthinkable before Katrina wreaked havoc on the Big Easy. To be sure, there is still a long distance to go. But something is going right in New Orleans.

Why the success? It's all about three things: (1) removing barriers to change; (2) having a coherent coordinated approach to an array of multiple thoughtful strategies; and (3) adapting to the outcomes—what doesn't work, *dump*, and what does work, *expand*.

Katrina brought with it a series of coincidences and courage. Though deadly and devastating, Katrina essentially created the conditions necessary to knock down the barriers to change; then Democratic governor Kathleen Blanco courageously acted in the breach and rescued the chronically failing schools from district control with the idea that all schools would be charter schools. She added courage on courage and refused to impose a complicated and crippling collective-bargaining agreement on the RSD. Following suit, the school board boldly chartered most of its high-performing schools and it too rejected a new collective-bargaining agreement.

The governor and school board offered a new vision—build a decentralized school district where schools were empowered to decide how to educate children and were held rigorously accountable. But this still was insufficient. Many new, bold strategies were required to implement this vision. Data became the driver, charter schools were put out of business if they didn't cut it, community groups organized, nonprofits sprouted up, philanthropists invested, politicians supported, parents became educated purchasers, universities critiqued, newspapers editorialized—most embracing the vision and working consistently with it. Policies consistent with the vision were adopted—new funding formulas that allow money to follow the child, mechanisms to inform parents so they could make better choices, open enrollment, citywide registration, and better human capital strategies like rewarding successful educators and schools. Considerable time was spent to evaluate the coherence of these policies. Those proffered that did not support the vision had to be adapted or abandoned.

Essentially, Hess and Sattin-Bajaj's book contends that if you focus on one piece of the system and expect different outcomes, chances of your success are highly unlikely, and any success experienced certainly won't be widespread, consistent, or above average. Instead, for big results to occur, the work must be done across all elements of the system in a coordinated way. They posit that it could happen if some really big ideas written in their compendium were applied in a coherent way. I believe New Orleans' post-Katrina experience supports that notion. In the end, it is not necessary to have a Katrina to radically improve outcomes for students, as there are many ways to remove the barriers to change. The real test is the hard work of rethinking these systems, which is something that everyone everywhere can and should pursue. I only wish I'd had this book around in August 2006 and suggest that it be a manifesto to reformers not only in Milwaukee but also around the country.

Paul Pastorek
Chief Administrative Officer, Chief Counsel, and Corporate Secretary
EADS North America
Former State Superintendent of Education (2007–2011)
Louisiana Department of Education

Introduction

Frederick M. Hess, Carolyn Sattin-Bajaj,
and Taryn Hochleitner

This volume starts from a simple premise. Widely hyped school reforms of recent decades have too often disappointed, and a crucial reason is that "bold" calls for professionalism, accountability, and choice have amounted to little more than modest tweaks to the familiar routines of schools and systems. Disappointing outcomes are chalked up to "flawed implementation" or taken as a signal that it's time to try another promising reform. Yet this entire minuet—including those measures, like mayoral control, merit pay, or charter schooling, that are heralded (or castigated) as "radical"—typically leaves the familiar rhythms of schools, school districts, age-graded classrooms, and teacher job descriptions intact. Indeed, watching the efforts play out, it can seem that many reformers believe that merely appending merit pay, revamped teacher evaluation, increased parental choice, or new turnaround strategies to the aging architecture of schooling will be enough to set matters right.

Meanwhile, those skeptical of these more "radical" reforms tend to insist that the only viable path to improvement is more money and professional development. Needless to say, such measures, whatever their merits, leave untouched the shape and the norms of schools and systems. This book starts from the premise that the vast majority of efforts to drive improvement by spending more and providing more professional development have had a limited impact, at best. This is a book for those who seek a more promising path.

This is a book for those who think the status quo is inadequate, agree that decades of efforts to "reform" school systems have failed to significantly improve matters, and are seeking a more promising path forward. That's what the contributors offer in the chapters that follow.

Today, it can be easy for would-be reformers to lose sight of the fundamental changes needed to help realize their grand aims. For instance, reformers wax enthusiastic about merit pay, while leaving intact the traditional teacher's role, school staffing, and the organization of instruction. Indeed, today's "cutting-edge" merit-pay strategies, with bonuses based on movement in student test scores, typically assume an individual teacher will retain sole instructional responsibility for a group of students in a tested subject for 180 days. (Any other arrangement would call the underlying assumptions of the bonus system into doubt.) Rather than viewing pay reform as a tool for rethinking teaching, reformers wind up layering merit pay atop industrial-era pay scales. The result is a series of frustrations and disappointments.

In all of this, would-be reformers find themselves trying to design twenty-first-century schools upon the foundation of systems that were never designed to address today's challenges. Unlike sectors such as medicine, engineering, farming, or air travel, which look profoundly different today than they did a century ago, schools and schooling look remarkably like they did in 1920. In other sectors, dramatic shifts in the labor force, management practices, technology, and communications transformed familiar institutions and comfortable routines into more efficient and more effective versions of themselves. These transformative gains have generally not been a product of doing the same things in the same way, only "better" or with more elbow grease. Rather, they have been the result of rethinking the way the work is done.

Now, to be fair, in any sector, this kind of redesign and rethinking is usually not the handiwork of large, established organizations. In other sectors, reinvention is often the result of dynamic new ventures displacing the old. In schooling, however, this passing of the baton is largely absent. This means that more conscious, more purposive, action is essential if systems are to be retooled.

What this book offers is a series of incisive, highly readable strategies, penned by some of the nation's leading education thinkers, on what that kind of retooling will entail and how states and communities can start to put it into practice. Taken as a whole, the chapters seek to offer something akin to a blueprint for system change. Of course, such discussions can tend toward the airy and abstract. So, the contributors have sought to ground their guidance by broadly applying it to the concrete realities of one city—in this case, for reasons we'll discuss shortly, Milwaukee, Wisconsin.

The reform blueprint that follows consists of eight distinct, but complementary, "pillars" of reform: new school delivery, quality control, a recovery school district, professional practice, talent management, resource use, data collection, and effective governance. Together, these amount to the foundation for a comprehensive agenda of system transformation.

EIGHT PILLARS OF REFORM

The point here is not to introduce novel strategies or fanciful new jargon. Rather, the contributors offer clear-eyed thinking on how these things can be done profoundly better—often by approaching them in quite different ways than has been the norm. With that, let's briefly touch on each of the eight pillars, just to be clear on what each entails.

New Schools and Innovative Delivery: Today's "factory-model" schoolhouse reflects a presumption that students can be well served in age-graded classrooms of twenty or thirty students, with teachers doing their best to differentiate and meet each of their particular needs in the course of a 180-day academic year. New school formation focuses on creating room for schools that offer more personalized learning experiences, by employing customized school designs and digital learning. New school delivery is a question of leveraging new providers, alternative school models, and virtual schooling, with the district operating as a manager of a "portfolio" of schools.

Quality Control: Without an adequate system for tracking and controlling quality, welcoming new providers and different school designs can amount to an empty gesture. The point here is to move beyond stale debates about No Child Left Behind–style accountability and instead embrace a more robust notion of quality control that's suited to a diverse array of schools and education providers. This requires identifying the right combination of input regulations, outcome metrics, and market signals to create a dynamic environment in which mediocrity is addressed and high performers are encouraged to thrive.

Recovery School District: Frustration with ineffectual efforts to improve persistently troubled schools has led state and district leaders to look for more forceful strategies. In many cases, this requires new governance structures equal to the task. One vehicle for doing this is the Recovery School District (RSD). Special statewide districts tasked with transforming troubled schools, RSDs don't operate schools. Instead, they leverage a variety of school providers, traditional and charter. Making this work is not merely a question of governance, but also of recruiting new talent, installing quality leadership, and setting the conditions for sustained success.

Professional Practice: Regardless of the school model in question, the quality of teaching is going to determine whether students are learning. This is why professional development is such a major component of any improvement strategy. Yet, this work tends to take the form of "drive-by" workshops that too often yield little meaningful change in teacher practice. Getting professional practice right requires not just a new set of trainers or training practices, but also a fundamentally different mindset.

Talent Management: Identifying and attracting high-quality talent to the teaching profession goes hand-in-hand with efforts to improve the work of those already in the system. But "improving teacher quality" is often more an exhortation than a plan for action. Getting better at "talent management"— including how to recruit, evaluate, and retain professionals—is a key piece of any transformative strategy. This includes rethinking how to structure compensation, training, and career ladders.

Resource Allocation: In an era of tight budgets, finding the money to fuel improvement is a challenge. This requires eliminating wasteful outlays and steering dollars to places where they'll have the biggest impact. Careful stewardship and strategic planning are critical here, including a willingness to carefully scour expenditures and map them against priorities.

Harnessing Data and Analytics: In school systems that feature multiple school models and providers, parents need better access to clear, helpful information to help them make good choices. States and districts can start to better utilize already-available data to make strategic management decisions. Creating mechanisms through which to produce, analyze, and share data is an indispensible tool in a transformative reform agenda.

Governance and System Leadership: Transformative change requires leadership that can bring coherence to the work of changing policy and practice on multiple fronts. While strategic planning is important, more vital is the kind of leadership that can hold the course in the face of structural challenges and political opposition. This entails negotiating changes to collective-bargaining agreements, making unpopular personnel adjustments, and partnering with outside funders and community players. Leaders need the stamina to not just break ground on the construction of new systems but also see the work through to fruition.

WHY THIS BOOK?

Let's be clear. This volume is hardly the first attempt to tackle the subject of system reform. Many have chronicled ambitious endeavors to reform school systems or proposed strategies for system improvement. Many of these works are valuable and insightful. But we think the present volume is distinct from much of what has come before.

The existing works that may most resemble this one are part of a decade-old trilogy—*Fixing Urban Schools*, *It Takes a City: Getting Serious about Urban School Reform*, and *Making School Reform Work: New Partnerships for Real Change*.[1] Those volumes, penned by education researcher Paul Hill and a variety of colleagues, sought to sketch the challenges of urban system reform and the kinds of leadership and activity that would deliver transformative improvement. The biggest difference between our effort and that one may be that those volumes sought to address the world of school reform circa 2000, when the policy, data, and technology landscape looked profoundly different than it does today. We hope this volume will offer to today's readers what those books offered to their counterparts ten or fifteen years ago.

A larger body of existing work has sought to pinpoint deficiencies in existing urban and system reform efforts, drawing out lessons learned from particular districts. In *So Much Reform, So Little Change: The Persistence of Failure in Urban Schools*, University of Chicago professor Charles Payne dissects thirty years of unsuccessful reform in the Windy City. In a similar effort, Claremont University's Charles Taylor Kerchner and his colleagues examine four decades of reform in Los Angeles in *Learning from L.A.: Institutional Change in American Public Education*.[2] Other volumes in this genre include *As Good as It Gets: What School Reform Brought to Austin*; *Education Reform in New York City: Ambitious Change in the Nation's Most Complex School System*; and *Urban School Reform: Lessons from San Diego*.[3] These terrific volumes illustrate how school reform efforts have played out in particular communities, and can help inform decision-making in any district. Of course, by design, these volumes tend to focus on understanding what has happened and not on articulating a forward-looking vision.

Another body of work offers holistic pedagogical advice on system reform. Books like former deputy minister of Ontario Ben Levin's *How to Change 5000 Schools: A Practical and Positive Approach for Leading Change at Every Level*; Michel Fullan's *All Systems Go: The Change Imperative for Whole System Reform*; and Michael Barber, Andy Moffit, and Paul Kihn's *Deliverology 101: A Field Guide for Educational Leaders* tend to focus on culture-building, instruction, and organizational routine.[4] These authors are less focused on the work our contributors tackle here, which is how to reshape district institutions and routines. These works and the contributions that follow can best be read as complements; the blueprint sketched here is intended to leave educators better positioned to pursue the instructional and organizational guidance our authors provide.

A third set of works features volumes that tackle one specific element of school improvement. Some volumes focus on finance, like Allan Odden and Lawrence Picus's *School Finance: A Policy Perspective*, Marguerite Roza's *Educational Economics: Where Do School Funds Go?*, or Frederick M. Hess and Eric Osberg's *Stretching the School Dollar*.[5] Others focus on professional development, like Marsha Speck and Carol Knipe's *Why Can't We Get It Right?: Designing High-Quality Professional Development for Standards-Based Schools*.[6] A terrific recent contribution to this body of work is Andy Smarick's volume on governance and choice, *The Urban School System of the Future*. But even that ambitious work only touches on a select number of the pillars and does not attempt to wade into areas like professional practice or talent development. Works like these can best be understood as complementing and enriching the thinking on each of the enumerated pillars. What's distinctive here is especially the opportunity to think about how these various improvement strategies may complement one another.

What we seek to do differently here is sketch an integrated, coherent blueprint that approaches key components of system reform. The chapters that follow will clearly address not only what actions need to be taken but also the types of policy changes needed if those measures are to succeed.

WHY MILWAUKEE?

Discussed in the abstract, each of the eight pillars can seem vague, platitudinous, or a little fuzzy. For that reason, we've asked the contributors to use the city of Milwaukee as a case where they can sketch out particulars of what their proposals might look like in practice. While every school system is unique, Milwaukee is an intriguing example of a large city where one finds disappointing test scores and graduation rates, widespread school choice, budgetary woes, and a dynamic political and policy environment. That all seemed to add up to an inviting laboratory for fresh thinking.

Milwaukee may be best known in education circles for being the site of the nation's pioneering school voucher program, which began more than two decades ago. Today, the city is dotted with a variety of schools, including an array of private schools participating in the public voucher program and charter schools authorized by a variety of entities, including the University of Wisconsin–Milwaukee and the city of Milwaukee.

In 1990, the city of Milwaukee established the Milwaukee Parental Choice Program (MPCP), the nation's first school voucher program.[7] The MPCP made low-income students eligible for publicly funded vouchers that cover private-school tuition at over one hundred participating schools. Today, over 23,000 Milwaukee students participate in the MPCP, receiving a voucher worth more than $6,000. Private-school vouchers represent only one of the kinds of choices that families have in Milwaukee. Wisconsin was an early adopter of charter-school legislation, and today there are more than two hundred charter schools in the state, with multiple charter authorizers operating in Milwaukee alone. Since the 1970s, Wisconsin has also featured an open enrollment policy, allowing minority students to enroll in neighboring suburban districts.

Milwaukee Public Schools (MPS) has also featured a host of attempted system reforms in recent decades. Since a push for decentralization and greater school-based autonomy in the early 1990s, reforms have included efforts to promote smaller schools, accountability and assessment, and, more recently, a district-wide instructional-improvement plan. Over two decades, MPS has seen more than its share of superintendents and reform agendas.[8]

For all of this activity, student achievement and graduation rates have failed to show much movement. According to the 2011 Trial Urban District Assessment (a district-level analysis of the National Assessment of Education Progress), just 10 percent of Milwaukee eighth-graders are proficient in math and just 12 percent in reading.[9]

Like so many systems, reformers in Milwaukee have tended to graft innovative approaches onto antiquated systems. Little has been done to redesign human resources, budgeting, data, or quality-control systems to meet the opportunities of a new era. Attempts to create potential linkages among the district-, charter-, and private-school sectors have been sparse, and the few tentative efforts haven't amounted to much.

These frustrations are not inevitable. Twenty-first-century school reform presents new opportunities to revisit old assumptions. For better and worse, the Wisconsin legislature's 2011 passage of Act 10 ensured that Wisconsin's school systems would have the chance to rethink old rules governing schools and classrooms. By limiting collective bargaining and changing pension, healthcare, and retirement obligations, it freed up hundreds of millions in funds, creating a windfall that can support schools, classrooms, instruction, and teachers. In 2012, the highly touted Rocketship Academies selected Milwaukee as one of the first places outside of California where it would open its "hybrid" (i.e., technology-infused) school model. Wisconsin received a federal waiver from many of the more burdensome requirements of No Child Left Behind, opening the door to a smarter accountability system.

In other words, like so many other places, Milwaukee is at a crossroads: it can build a dynamic, quality-focused entrepreneurial ecosystem that allows problem-solvers to emerge, or it can continue to meander along the familiar path of pursuing reforms under which nothing much ever changes. In short, Milwaukee provides a terrific opportunity for the contributors to explain how the key pillars of transformative reform might play out.

THE BOOK AHEAD

The contributors to this project represent an impressive collection of thinkers and doers, who here collaborate to sketch a blueprint for transforming America's school systems. They don't just offer a few pet proposals; rather, they explain how to reform a district's educational ecosystem, including human capital, professional development, resource allocation, choice and innovation, and research and development.

In chapter 1, Michael B. Horn, cofounder and executive director of the California-based Clayton Christensen Institute for Disruptive Innovation and coauthor of *Disrupting Class*, and his colleague Meg Evans tackle the question of new schools and innovative delivery. They suggest that creating a dynamic environment for educational innovation requires that districts must move away from their traditional role as direct operator of identical schools. Instead, districts need to embrace a role in which they operate as manager of a diverse collection of school types and support services. Horn and Evans describe the means necessary for this shift, and discuss ways in which districts and schools can incorporate technology to facilitate customization for students.

In chapter 2, Thomas B. Fordham Institute vice president Michael J. Petrilli tackles the vital challenge of rigorous but flexible quality control. Petrilli explains how the three main quality-control tools used by policymakers today—input and process regulation, outcome-based accountability, and market-based signaling—can more effectively and powerfully be employed in concert, for a variety of providers.

In chapter 3, Neerav Kingsland, chief executive officer of New Schools for New Orleans, describes the essential features of a Recovery School District. Drawing on his deep knowledge of the challenges and successes of Louisiana's Recovery School District, Kingsland describes the ways in which RSDs can improve student achievement by acting as market creators, ambassadors, and bankruptcy stewards. He also discusses the type of policy environment, leadership, and community support needed to successfully develop and launch an RSD.

In chapter 4, Doug Lemov, bestselling author of *Teach Like a Champion* and cofounder of Uncommon Schools, sketches a powerful new vision for how to organize and deliver professional development. He calls for a model of "professional practice" that relies on school leaders to identify their best teachers; to study what these teachers do to make a difference for kids; and to then leverage this information to help other teachers improve their performance through mentoring, ongoing feedback, and communal practice.

In chapter 5, Dr. Ranjit Nair, assistant professor of management at St. Edward's University, notes that school improvement turns on the quality of the people in classrooms and schools—but that most districts lack the kinds of talent management and HR systems they need. Speaking from his experience as a high-ranking HR executive at the Bank of America and Honeywell International, Nair sketches a strategy for strengthening human-capital management that incorporates enhanced recruitment techniques, increased rigor in performance management, and strategically aligned compensation schemes.

In chapter 6, Jonathan Travers, Genevieve Green, and Karen Hawley Miles of Education Resource Strategies tackle the issue of efficient management of financial capital. Schools and system are wrestling with the realities of tight budgets and limited resources. This means that transformative improvement requires finding new ways to target resources, identify waste, and invest scarce funds. The authors sketch a four-part strategy to guide that process.

In chapter 7, Jon Fullerton, executive director of Harvard University's Center for Education Policy Research, offers guidance on how states and systems can forge a research and development system that empowers districts to improve their practices and outcomes. Although states, districts, charter-school networks, and individual private and public schools today collect vast amounts of data, these data are rarely organized or analyzed in ways that support strategic decision-making or policy design. Fullerton specifies a series of changes in policy and practice that can turn things around.

In chapter 8, Heather Zavadsky, author of *Building School Reform to Scale: Five Exemplary Urban Districts* and *School Turnarounds: The Essential Role of Districts*, presents a model for thinking about effective district governance and management. The various moving pieces of reform only work well when a school district pursues them in a coherent fashion. And that requires strategic leadership. Zavadsky draws on lessons learned from successful superintendents and districts to offer some tenets to guide system reform.

In the conclusion, we'll have a few words to say about the takeaways and how practitioners, policymakers, parents, and philanthropists can start to put all of this to work.

Well-intended reform efforts have a disappointing record when it comes to delivering on their grand ambitions. The chapters that follow start from the premise that much of this record is due to a failure to recognize what it will take to fundamentally redesign existing schools and systems if they are to be equal to the challenges of the twenty-first century.

The ensuing pages seek to sketch a blueprint for such an effort. Years of grand promises and disappointing results have soured many communities on overhyped visions of reform. What we hope is notable about the blueprint offered here is that it is neither airy nor larded with sugarplum promises. The recommendations here will not deliver miracle cures. But they can help to create the kind of system in which great educators can thrive, can get the kind of support they need, and are held accountable in more sensible and appropriate ways. In doing that, we believe they can set the foundations for transformative improvement in the years ahead.

NOTES

1. Paul T. Hill and Mary Beth Celio, *Fixing Urban Schools* (Washington, DC: Brookings Institution Press, 1998); Paul T. Hill, James Harvey, Christine Campbell, and Carol Reed, *It Takes a City: Getting Serious about Urban School Reform* (Washington, DC: Brookings Institution Press, 1999); Paul T. Hill and James Harvey Jr., *Making School Reform Work: New Partnerships for Real Change* (Washington, DC: Brookings Institution Press, 2004).

2. Charles M. Payne, *So Much Reform, So Little Change: The Persistence of Failure in Urban Schools* (Cambridge: Harvard Education Press, 2008); Charles T. Kerchner et al., *Learning from L.A.: Institutional Change in American Public Education* (Cambridge: Harvard Education Press, 2008).

3. Larry Cuban, *As Good As It Gets: What School Reform Brought to Austin* (Cambridge: Harvard University Press, 2010); Jennifer O'Day, Catherine Bitter, and Louis Gomez, *Education Reform in New York City: Ambitious Change in the Nation's Most Complex School System* (Cambridge: Harvard Education Press, 2011); Frederick M. Hess, *Urban School Reform: Lessons from San Diego* (Cambridge: Harvard Educational Press, 2005).

4. Ben Levin, *How to Change 5000 Schools: A Practical and Positive Approach for Leading Change at Every Level* (Cambridge: Harvard Education Press, 2008); Michel Fullan, *All Systems Go: The Change Imperative for Whole System Reform* (Thousand Oaks, CA: Corwin, 2010); Michael Barber, Andy Moffit, and Paul Kihn, *Deliverology 101: A Field Guide for Educational Leaders* (Thousand Oaks, CA: Corwin, 2010).

5. Allan Odden and Lawrence Picus, *School Finance: A Policy Perspective* (New York: McGraw-Hill, 2007); Marguerite Roza, *Educational Economics: Where Do School Funds Go?* (Washington, DC: Urban Institute Press, 2010); Frederick M. Hess and Eric Osberg, *Stretching the School Dollar: How Schools and Districts Can Save Money while Serving Students Best* (Cambridge: Harvard Education Press, 2010).

6. Marsha Speck and Caroll Knipe, *Why Can't We Get It Right?: Designing High-Quality Professional Development for Standards-Based Schools* (Thousand Oaks, CA: Corwin, 2005).

7. Frederick M. Hess, *Revolution at the Margins: The Impact of Competition on Urban School Systems* (Washington, DC: Brookings Institution Press, 2002); John F. Witte, *The Market Approach to Education: An Analysis of America's First Voucher Program* (Princeton, NJ: Princeton University Press, 2001).

8. Ken Montgomery, Linda Darling-Hammond, and Carol Campbell, *Developing Common Instructional Practice across a Portfolio of Schools: The Evolution of School Reform in Milwaukee* (Stanford, CA: Stanford University, Stanford Center for Opportunity Policy in Education, 2011).

9. The Nation's Report Card, "Trial Urban District Assessment," 2013, www.nationsreportcard.gov (accessed January 21, 2013).

Chapter One

New Schools and Innovative Delivery

Michael B. Horn and Meg Evans

The past several decades have seen technology transform industry after industry. Nearly every sector in America has used new technologies to innovate in ways nearly unimaginable a generation ago. By the term *technology*, we refer to the processes by which an organization transforms labor, capital, materials, and information into products and services of greater value. The notion is not limited to things like microprocessors and other electronics. Innovation in this context refers to a change in one of these technologies. [1]

One sector, however, has remained nearly the same as it was a century ago. The American school system has continued to rely on an anachronistic factory-based model, even as so much of society has transformed around it. To the extent that it has employed technology, it has done so to sustain and reinforce its factory-model processes, not to fundamentally change them.

That urban school districts in particular have long struggled to innovate beyond their factory-based model is not news. School principals and teachers complain frequently of top-down control from the district central office, which fosters a culture of compliance rather than one of innovation and pursuing different strategies for different student populations. Many district administrators have historically worried that if they give more autonomy to schools, only chaos will result and students will not be served well.

Milwaukee provides a case study with which to understand the tensions around welcoming innovation—or even making basic progress—that are so common in urban school districts around the nation. District teachers complain about wanting to implement various new ideas, such as offering new curricula to serve certain students or creating after-school programs, but being blocked for reasons having to do with central control. According to focus-group interviews with Milwaukee teachers, receiving a mid-year mandate from the district staff to implement a specific curriculum or a district-wide order to switch to forty-eight-minute periods from eighty-minute periods—regardless of what the school itself sees as best for its students—is not out of the ordinary.[2] Innovation hardly enters the conversation.

Milwaukee does have a relatively long history of school choice and a variety of autonomous schools from which students can choose. This creates the context for an innovative model that offers a suite of options to best fit individual student needs. However, the district itself has not adopted a mindset of viewing these and its own traditional schools as a portfolio of options for students. As in many urban districts, a top-down mindset seems to have prevailed. Although some of Milwaukee's past superintendents have seen technology—in the form of computers and e-learning, for example—as a critical part of their strategy and invested accordingly, others have come in and let the investments wane. Neither consistency nor individual school autonomy appears to be in long supply.

Complaints of heavy bureaucracies stifling innovation in education are, of course, nothing new. The culture that has squelched innovation in urban school districts—embedded in both explicit and implicit processes—should not come as a surprise.[3] A series of accompanying policies, regulations, and agreements to govern and manage today's education system has emerged over the last several decades that, until more recently, has focused largely on controlling inputs as opposed to student outcomes.

These inputs control both the resources and the processes inside schools. They include things like teacher-certification laws, which in essence dictate the population from which schools can hire teachers, and categorical funding that locks in place the things on which schools can and cannot spend money. Managing an urban school district through such inputs threatens to restrict and block innovation. If one were to specify all of the inputs into a meal in advance, for example—the ingredients and what to do with them—the odds of someone creating something different and innovative would be low, as the solution would have been essentially defined beforehand.[4]

The same principle is at work in places like Milwaukee and many urban school districts around the nation. Focusing on inputs has the effect of locking a system into a set way of doing things and inhibiting innovation. Focusing on outcomes, on the other hand, encourages continuous improvement against an overall set of goals.

None of this would be quite so problematic were it not for the fact that the school system we have was not built to deliver for society's needs today.

MOVING BEYOND A MONOLITHIC EDUCATION SYSTEM

The systems in place in urban school districts around the country were created in the early 1900s to serve a different time with different needs. Only 50 percent of five- to nineteen-year-olds were enrolled in school in 1900. One-third of children enrolled in first grade made it to high school and of those, only one-third graduated.[5]

Competition with a fast-rising industrial Germany changed that as Americans asked public education to prepare everyone for a vocation in the Industrial Age of factories. To do this, the school system changed gears and adopted a factory model that allowed it to extend high school to everyone in an efficient, affordable manner. In just one generation, America built a comprehensive high school system that enrolled 75 percent of the students who had started in first grade and graduated 45 percent of them.

That number continued to rise throughout most of the century, although in the nation's largest fifty cities, it has remained stuck just above 50 percent. Milwaukee fits the bill, as it graduated 50 percent of its students in 1997,[6] a number that rose to 62.8 percent by 2011, although the rate of growth has slowed as of late.[7]

The factory-model system that educators adopted created schools that in essence monolithically processed students in batches. By instituting grades and having a teacher focus on just one set of students of the same academic proficiency, the theory went, teachers could teach "the same subjects, in the same way and at the same pace" to all children in the classroom.[8] This created a school system that is built to standardize the way students are taught and tested.

When most students would grow up to work in a factory or an industrial job of some sort, this standardization worked just fine. But now that we ask increasingly more students to master higher-order knowledge and skills—in 1900, only 17 percent of all jobs required so-called knowledge workers, whereas over 60 percent do today—this arrangement falls short.[9] Wisconsin and Milwaukee have felt this pressure acutely. Between 2011 and 2012 Wisconsin had the biggest six-month decline in manufacturing jobs in the nation after California.[10] According to a *Milwaukee Journal Sentinel* special report, the city's pool of college-educated adults ranks among the lowest of the country's fifty biggest cities.[11] To become an average city among the top fifty, Milwaukee would need another thirty-six thousand adults with college degrees. Since 1990, it has added fewer than one thousand a year. And Milwaukee is not alone in facing such a formidable gap between supply and demand for highly educated professionals.

The reason the factory-model education system that standardizes will not work given these new needs is, to put it simply, because everyone has different learning needs at different times. We learn at different paces, have different aptitudes, and enter classes with different experiences and background knowledge. Because of this, each child needs a different, customized learning approach to maximize his or her potential.

This need for customization clashes directly with today's factory-model school system, which was built to standardize. When a class or teacher is ready to move on to a new concept today, all students move on, regardless of how many have mastered the previous concept (even if it is a prerequisite for learning what is next). On the other hand, if some students are able to master a course in just a few weeks, they remain in the class for the whole semester. Both the bored and the bewildered see their opportunity to achieve shredded by the system.

To customize in the monolithic education system we have today is prohibitively expensive. Just witness how much more it costs to educate a special-needs student with an individualized learning plan—two to three times, on average. As a result, over the last three decades, special education has sucked up more and more funds and made the overall system more and more unaffordable without the overall results to show for it.[12] In many districts, special education now accounts for over a third of the spending.[13] In Milwaukee, for example, 19.7 percent of students were classified as special education in 2011–2012.[14] In the FY13 proposed budget, special-education services to schools account for roughly 20 percent of the operating funds and 16 percent of the total budget.[15]

Milwaukee and urban school districts across the nation must embrace innovation to break out of this monolithic education system. There are several innovations that many urban districts have begun to put in place that hold promise, and there are many more that they should implement in the years ahead.

INNOVATING TOWARD A STUDENT-CENTRIC EDUCATION SYSTEM

Urban school districts must innovate across two parallel paths: with new whole-school models and within schools.

Innovating with New Whole-School Models

The first path of innovation requires that districts adopt a mindset in which they see themselves as overseeing a portfolio of different types of schools, rather than running a set of similar "one-size-fits-all" schools.[16] A growing number of urban school districts, including New York, Los Angeles, and Denver, have begun to adopt this portfolio approach. In many ways, the city of Milwaukee has also operated with a portfolio of school types for students for many years, as it has a variety of autonomous schools from which students can choose, including charter schools under the purview of different authorizers, magnet schools, private choice schools funded through vouchers, and traditional district schools.

But the district itself has not traditionally viewed these, along with its own traditional schools, as a portfolio of options for students. Instead, historically speaking, the district seems to have viewed choice schools of nearly all stripes as threats to its existing business model, as its share of per-pupil funds declines with students attending nondistrict choice schools. Judging from focus groups with parents, having this perspective has only sown seeds of confusion and created a series of systems that have frustrated students' ability to find the education that is right for them. Parents receive only a simple booklet at the start of the year listing all of the district schools with brief descriptions and test-score metrics, and they struggle to understand which school might be the best fit for their child.

Having different school types available for different students is critical, as not all school architectures can serve all students with differing needs. Just because two students live a block apart does not mean they automatically have the same needs, and yet the geographic categorization in use in many urban school districts suggests that we think they do.

The success of charter schools like KIPP helps reveal this: KIPP has created a school that works well for certain types of students, many of whom have struggled in traditional schools, but it is unlikely that KIPP is the right fit for all students. This is one critical reason to move toward a portfolio of school options and to allow for innovation in creating and welcoming new school architectures designed to serve different student needs.

Moving to this portfolio mindset requires significant business-model innovation for both the district and individual schools, as it requires the district to shift from running schools to instead seeing itself as an authorizer of schools and purveyor of supporting school services.[17] Operationally, this means allowing schools to control their own budgets, hiring, and curriculum planning. This shift from top-down choices to ground-level control returns the decisions about what's best for students to those closest to the classroom. Rather than viewing their charge as preserving the public schools in their geographical jurisdiction, public school boards and superintendents must view their mission as educating well all the students within that area.

A critical function in this new model is that the district move beyond input-based standards that seek to dictate how schools teach students, which are anathema to innovation, and instead create outcome-based student-growth standards to give innovators a common target toward which to improve. For example, rather than mandating on the district-level that a school or teacher uses a particular literacy curriculum, the state should instead require students to make, at minimum, a one grade level gain in reading level over the course of the year and then let the teacher decide the best way to facilitate that growth.

Much as in a Recovery School District of the type Neerav Kingsland proposes (this volume), the district's job would be both to shut down schools

over time that do not perform up to par and to help parents and students find
the right school for their needs, thereby framing the creation of new schools
as a constant chance for innovation to learn which types of schools serve
which types of students best—and to acknowledge that no school will likely
serve all students well.[18] This shift is dramatic. Districts have long defended
and made excuses for failing neighborhood schools; instead they ought to
hold all of the schools in their purview—magnet, charter, traditional, and
alternative—to the same standards and review processes. If any school is
continuously failing students, the district should take swift action.

That this will be a significant shift in business model is evident in what
has played out in Milwaukee. Although the city has experienced the job of
shutting down poor schools already, this experience does not largely reside
inside the district, as reports indicate that it is the choice schools outside of
the district's management that have been held to a higher standard and closed
more quickly than their district-school counterparts. Indeed, the district and
the various organizations and associations tied into its operations have instead created caps on nonunionized district schools—non-MPS providers are
allowed to serve only 8 percent of the district's total enrollment—which
blocks innovation and does not foster an ecosystem of continuous improvement around student outcomes.[19]

This also requires schools to rethink their business model, as, increasingly, rather than being operating units within the district, they will be autonomous business models themselves. For this to work, rather than have dollars
flow to districts that make decisions as to their allocation, dollars must follow
students down to the school—or better yet, follow students to the educational
experience—of their choice.

In other words, the school-level leadership must have the ability to make
financial, human resource, curricular, and other operational decisions on its
own.[20] The choice and charter schools in Milwaukee have some experience
with this already, as they have significantly more flexibility than the traditional district schools in making curricular and architectural choices for their
students, creating ways to work with parents, and establishing new processes
to work one-on-one with students.[21]

The district should also embrace the power of disruptive innovation in
seeding new school models. A disruptive innovation is an innovation that
transforms a sector that was once characterized by complicated, expensive,
and inaccessible products and services into one where the products and services are more affordable, simple, and convenient. There are two critical
enablers of disruptive innovations: a business-model innovation and a technology enabler that allows the innovation to carry a low-cost business model
up-market to serve more and more demanding users.

Blended-learning, or hybrid, schools that combine online learning with
elements of a brick-and-mortar experience have the potential to serve this

purpose and be disruptive relative to the first generation of "no excuses" charter schools, for example, by being lower in cost and therefore theoretically easier to scale. Milwaukee has a few blended-learning schools and pilot programs in operation, and the community has welcomed Rocketship Education, a charter-management organization that runs disruptive blended-learning schools relative to first-generation charter schools. As urban districts around the country move to a portfolio model, they should seek to bring Rocketship and other similar disruptive blended-learning school models to their district as well.

Driving Innovation within Schools

Urban districts must also embrace the use of technology to transform the learning environments within schools themselves and allow for a much finer grain of educational customization for students than is possible at the whole-school level.[22] For far too long, urban districts have deployed technology by simply cramming it into their existing schools and classrooms as an add-on or small supplement—and have spent not insignificant sums in doing so. For example, Milwaukee has spent roughly 1 percent of its operating budget on technology over the last decade, but it is not clear that those investments have resulted in learning gains for students. Too many districts have historically mistaken an investment in technology for a thoughtful and strategic focus on innovation.

Instead, the district must use technology, specifically online learning, to disrupt the factory model of schooling and customize for students' different learning needs. Online learning appears to be a classic disruptive innovation, and it has the potential to not just help reform education but also transform it. Because it is inherently modular, it can more easily be customized for different student-learning needs than can the traditional classroom. It can also create near-real-time feedback loops to bolster the interactions with both the teacher and the content itself. The technology underlying it is beginning to improve year after year, and it has gained traction by targeting classic areas of nonconsumption, that is, where the alternative is literally nothing at all and where disruptive innovations get their start.

Milwaukee, like many urban districts, has some experience deploying online learning in these areas of nonconsumption—such as to offer advanced courses or extracurricular courses to students where the alternative in the home school has been nothing at all, or—most popularly—for credit recovery. But the schools and the district have not made as strategic use of these resources as they could to drive student learning.

Milwaukee, for example, had historically used online learning well in a handful of partnership or alternative schools to help serve students who had dropped out or were on the verge of doing so. More recently, the district has begun phasing these schools out—from twenty-one schools down to six—to the detriment of the students who now have no option to continue their schooling.[23] Furthermore, many urban districts like Milwaukee have ignored the potential to use online learning to implement blended-learning rotation models in elementary school classrooms.[24] Such models generally do not require significant redesign but can bolster student learning by creating better-targeted individualized pathways for each student as well as better uses of time and richer student-teacher interactions.

PRACTICAL IMPLICATIONS

To move toward an urban school district that uses innovation to improve student learning, districts and the states in which they operate should take several concrete steps.

Creating a Diverse Ecosystem

Urban districts must move toward a system of operating a portfolio of schools with a diversity of school types and a focus on student outcomes, not mandating how schools should best serve their students. Many urban districts across the country are moving in this direction.

Steps like Wisconsin's Act 114, a statewide bill that provided parents with an expanded window to take advantage of open enrollment and send their children to schools outside their districts, are important. A lesser-known aspect of this legislation also makes transferring possible mid-year if there is evidence that a student feels unsafe in her home school. Additionally, the current Milwaukee teachers union contract contains a cap on district-authorized, nonunion school enrollment. When this contract expires in July 2013, the cap will disappear with it. This presents an excellent opportunity to continue to develop the diverse ecosystem of choice for Milwaukee students with an expansion of charter and choice enrollment.

Urban districts moving into an authorizing role should also think about opening up umbrella charters to those organizations with a successful track record, so that innovative charter-management organizations looking to expand, such as Rocketship Education, will find these locales attractive places to put down roots.

Performance-Based Procurement

States like Florida and Utah have already created mechanisms through which to pay online-learning providers in part based on student outcomes. For example, in Utah, an online-learning provider receives 50 percent of funds up front for serving students but only receives the other 50 percent when a student successfully completes a course. This helps align incentives around actual student learning. Wisconsin should move forward with this type of policy—and where possible define successful student learning based on their passing objective, on-demand performance assessments.

But urban districts can themselves enter into performance-based contracts now without waiting for the legislature to act. Recently McGraw-Hill announced that it had entered into a performance-based contract with Western Governors University for its higher-education content, which suggests that even traditional textbook publishers might be open to these sorts of innovative contracts. Districts could offer the schools they authorize the opportunity to enter into different sorts of these arrangements with different vendors.

Funding Ecosystem

Lifting categorical funding requirements and the mandating of inputs at all levels and allowing funds to follow students down to the educational experience are critical. For urban districts coping with increasing budget cuts, allowing schools to have both more flexibility and the ability to opt in to performance-based contracts or other services that the district provides can help provide a gateway to innovative schooling arrangements. Such arrangements are more cost-effective and can achieve success for students, as several blended-learning proof points have shown across the nation.

In Milwaukee for example, almost a quarter of MPS's 9,300 employees are eligible for retirement, and the district estimates that more than 1,400 employees will retire by 2015.[25] This presents an ideal opportunity to not mandate that the district and its schools hire precise replacements, but to instead allow schools to create innovative staffing models and create blended-learning models that make sense for their needs.

Internet Connectivity

To support a move to blended learning, districts will also have to help schools have the proper Internet connectivity, as well as work with cities to ensure that students have adequate Internet access. Currently, most schools do not have adequate infrastructure to support Internet access, and many low-income residents do not have access to high-speed Internet. For example, according to interviews, in Milwaukee, Time-Warner Cable's monopoly has created expensive service that has limited student Internet access. Districts and states should use their potential scale to negotiate good contracts that schools can opt into and provide expertise to help schools implement and maintain their infrastructure wisely.

Building Broad-Based Community Support

Although structural changes are important, it is also important to gain buy-in from educators on the front lines who will be working directly with students—and to help educators see that the move to online and blended learning is not motivated by a desire to replace teachers with technology. Recently, the Rhode Island Department of Education held a large meeting for the district teachers, principals, parents, and administrators to establish a common language, understanding, and strategies for growth of digital learning in the state to spur educators on the front lines to lead the innovation.[26]

As urban districts move to a portfolio model of schooling, they ought to move into this educational role for educators as well and hold similar sessions. In many cases, this should spur immediate action, as educators in elementary schools in particular can establish blended-learning rotation models within their existing classrooms to better serve students. In addition, as Rhode Island did, urban districts ought to partner with interested foundations to establish competitive grants for educators and schools that create innovative school designs to bolster student outcomes.

Given that the teachers in Milwaukee were not even familiar with Wisconsin's plans on how to move to the Common Core standards or to adopt the SMARTER Balanced Assessment Consortium's new assessments, the importance of playing this educational role and holding sessions where appropriate cannot be overstated.

Move Away from Seat Time to a Competency-Based System

To bolster the likelihood that as educators adopt blended learning, this does not merely maintain the current factory-model system but in fact transforms it into a student-centric one, it is imperative that the state move beyond seat-time policies and create room for competency-based learning ones in which students make progress based on actual mastery of learning objectives.

In Milwaukee, blended-learning schools such as Milwaukee Community Cyber High School have managed to skirt seat-time requirements by chartering as virtual schools with the district—a clever way around the regulations but also far from ideal given that the Milwaukee Community Cyber High School is not in fact a full-time virtual school. Wisconsin ought to lift its existing seat-time requirements so that district schools that are not chartered as virtual schools can take advantage of competency-based learning as well. All states should have this mindset. This change requires state-level legislative action to change the educational code, but without community and thought leaders behind the change, there will likely be little impetus for legislators to take up the cause. For example, Utah passed a far-reaching bill to boost online learning in 2011 and allow it to escape the traditional seat-time metrics. To engineer this, a group of parents became active in lobbying for change, briefing each state senator, testifying at the committee level, and even hosting ice cream socials at the state capitol to raise awareness about the issue. The parents group also found it particularly helpful to have a couple of close allies in the Senate who stood as legislative champions of the cause.

Similarly, districts and states should move toward adopting or utilizing data and assessment systems that focus on individual student growth and allow students to move seamlessly between educational experiences, rather than treating students who enroll in different types of schools, for example, as separate silos of data. This practice, which is prevalent in Milwaukee, only creates complications for students and educators.[27]

CONCLUSION

Although urban school districts have struggled to innovate in the past, there is an opportunity to move beyond these struggles. With the rise of digital learning, there is a chance to transform the urban school district from its factory-model past into a student-centric system that can customize for each student's distinct learning needs and bolster each student's achievement.

Despite challenges that stand in the way of this change, there are concrete steps that state-level actors and district leaders can take to move toward this reality. From the low-hanging fruit of moving elementary schools to a station-rotation model and offering a wide range of individual online course options for high school students to the critical steps of removing seat-time requirements and focusing as a district on individual student-growth metrics, Milwaukee and other cities can begin to stand as models for the nation on how to capture the potential of online and blended learning.

Increasing numbers of charter networks and districts are grasping the promise of digital learning, but few have yet to reimagine and rebuild systematically with disruptive innovation in mind. Following the suggestions above, as well as engaging educators and the larger community, can begin a process of transformation that sets urban districts on a path to creating an education system markedly different from the one that has dominated the past century of education—and can help each child realize her fullest potential.

NOTES

1. Definitions are from Clayton M. Christensen's *The Innovator's Dilemma: When New Technologies Cause Great Firms to Fail* (Boston: Harvard Business School Press, 1997), introduction.

2. Will Howell interviewing a focus group of Milwaukee charter and choice teachers, July 12, 2012.

3. Edgar Schein, *Organizational Culture and Leadership* (San Francisco: Jossey-Bass, 1988), as summarized in the note by Clayton M. Christensen and Kirstin Shu, "What Is an Organization's Culture?," Harvard Business School Press, August 2, 2006.

4. See also Mike Petrilli's piece in this volume about quality control.

5. Clayton M. Christensen, Michael B. Horn, and Curtis W. Johnson, *Disrupting Class: How Disruptive Innovation Will Change the Way the World Learns* (New York: McGraw-Hill, 2008), 54.

6. Wisconsin Department of Public Instruction, WINSS Data Analysis, http://data.dpi. state.wi.us/data/HSCompletionPage.aspx?GraphFile=HIGHSCHOOLCOMPLETION& SCounty=47&SAthleticConf=45&SCESA=05&FULLKEY=01361903&SN=None+Chosen& DN=Milwaukee&OrgLevel=di&Qquad=performance.aspx&TmFrm=L (accessed July 25, 2012).

7. Note that this rate was calculated with the new Wisconsin Department of Public Instruction formula and may be lower than previous calculations. Using the legacy rate, this year's graduation rate would be measured as 68.6 percent.

8. Christensen, Horn, and Johnson, *Disrupting Class*, 35.

9. Patrick Butler et al., "A Revolution in Interaction," *McKinsey Quarterly* 1, no. 8 (1997), as cited in Michael E. Echols, *ROI on Human Capital Investment,* 2nd ed. (Arlington, VA: Tapestry Press, 2005), 3.

10. This is particularly significant because Wisconsin depends more on manufacturing for jobs than any state but Indiana. John Schmid and Craig Gilbert, "Wisconsin Missing Out on U.S. Job Gains," *Milwaukee Journal Sentinel,* March 3, 2012, www.jsonline.com/business/us-adding-jobs-while-state-loses-ll4c8qp-141333083.html (accessed July 25, 2012).

11. Rick Romell, "Does Milwaukee Have Enough College Graduates to Thrive?" *Milwaukee Journal Sentinel,* June 14, 2010, www.jsonline.com/business/96226434.html (accessed July 25, 2012).

12. See Jonathan Travers, Genevieve Green, and Karen Hawley Miles's piece in this volume for more on school-finance reform.

13. Stacey Childress and Stig Leschly, "Note on U.S. Public Education Finance (B): Expenditures," Harvard Business School Case Note, November 2, 2006, 5.

14. Wisconsin Department of Public Instruction, WINSS Data Analysis, http://data.dpi. state.wi.us/data/GroupEnroll.aspx?GraphFile=GROUPS&SCounty=47&SAthleticConf=45& SCESA=05&FULLKEY=01361903````&SN=None+Chosen&DN=Milwaukee&OrgLevel= di&Qquad=demographics.aspx&Group=Disability (accessed on August 15, 2012).

15. See the FY13 proposed budget at www2.milwaukee.k12.wi.us/portal/FY13/Supt_ Overview_2.pdf (accessed on August 2, 2012).

16. Paul T. Hill, "Put Learning First: A Portfolio Approach to Public Schools," Progressive Policy Institute Report, February 2006, www.eric.ed.gov/PDFS/ED491223.pdf (accessed May 16, 2013).

17. As Mark W. Johnson discusses in his book, *Seizing the White Space: Business Model Innovation for Growth and Renewal* (Boston: Harvard Business School Press, 2010), there are four elements of a business model—an organization's resources, processes, priorities, and value proposition. Understanding an organization's business model allows one to see what an organization is capable of doing, but also what it is not capable of doing. One of the central problems facing the education system is that, as alluded to earlier, it was built not to educate successfully each child but instead to offer something for everyone. Creating an education system designed to educate each student successfully requires significant business-model innovation.

18. See also Michael Petrilli's piece on quality control in this volume and Neerav Kingsland's piece on recovery school districts in this volume.

19. This cap is from a 1999 memo of understanding between the district and the Milwaukee Teachers Education Association. See Michael Ford, "MPS' Looming Fiscal Crack-up," *Wisconsin Interest* 21, no. 2 (June 2012), www.wpri.org/WIInterest/Vol21No2/Ford21.2.html (accessed July 25, 2012).

20. See Travers, Green, and Hawley Miles on school finance in this volume for more on bringing decision-making down to the school level.

21. One teacher in a Milwaukee choice school explained the power behind this approach in the following way: "Right now, we're in the process of rebuilding our own curriculums in whatever way we want to do it. Nothing's been defined, nothing's been laid out for us, they just expect results. And so we know that we have to work at a level to deliver excellent results. . . . We do have to be way more creative with the resources we have to make it happen, but our administration backs us a thousand percent, and we need it to make it happen." Focus group of Milwaukee charter and choice teachers, July 12, 2012.

22. For more on this, see Frederick M. Hess and Bruno V. Manno's *Customizing Schooling: Beyond Whole-School Reform* (Cambridge: Harvard Education Press, 2011).

23. Interview with Daniel Grego, executive director, TransCenter for Youth Inc., by Meg Evans, June 15, 2012.

24. *Blended learning* is defined in Michael B. Horn and Heather Staker's white paper, "Classifying Blended Learning," Innosight Institute, May 2012, on page 3 as "a formal education program in which a student learns at least in part through online delivery of content and instruction with some element of student control over time, place, path and/or pace and at least in part at a supervised brick-and-mortar location away from home." The rotation model is defined on page 8 as a program "in which within a given course or subject (e.g., math), students rotate on a fixed schedule or at the teacher's discretion between learning modalities, at least one of which is online learning. Other modalities might include activities such as small-group or full-class instruction, group projects, individual tutoring and pencil-and-paper assignments."

25. Ford, "MPS' Looming Fiscal Crack-up."

26. Meg Evans, "Convening Rhode Island around Digital Learning," Innosight Institute, June 2012.

27. See Jon Fullerton, this volume, for more on strategic uses of data.

Chapter Two

Quality Control in a Local Marketplace

Michael J. Petrilli

Quality control is the *sine qua non* of education reform. If this enterprise isn't about creating high-quality learning environments for students, what's the point? And in one sense, all of the topics covered in this volume—from funding to replication to governance and beyond—are about quality control: how to make it likelier that a community's portfolio of schools will be high-performing and lead to strong student outcomes.

This chapter can't cover all of that ground, so its focus will be somewhat narrower: What mix of policies, regulations, and organizational capacity can increase the likelihood that a local educational marketplace will be dominated by high-quality educational providers?

Quality control in an entrepreneurial sector presents special challenges. Our underlying premise is that competition and a significant degree of freedom can unleash innovation, creative problem-solving, and greater efficiency and effectiveness. (For more on unleashing innovation, see Horn and Evans, this volume.) Overdo the "control" part of "quality control," and policy-makers can squash this entrepreneurial energy. But simply "let a thousand flowers bloom" and leaders are unlikely to end up with the results they seek, as we learned in the early years of the national charter schools movement. As Frederick M. Hess put it in *Revolution at the Margins*, "Markets can be immensely powerful engines of social change, but they do not always produce the hoped-for outcomes."[1]

How, then, can policy-makers, philanthropists, and others involved in the design of educational marketplaces strike the right balance? And how is Milwaukee, in particular, doing on this score?

This chapter will argue that designers should be aiming for a thoughtful combination of input regulation, accountability for results, and robust market signals, as well as supply side support for schools and other providers. It will explore what that looks like for the district-, charter-, and private-school sectors, and will examine Milwaukee's strengths and weaknesses against that framework. Then it will explain how leaders—in Milwaukee and elsewhere—can move toward a robust quality-control environment.

QUALITY CONTROL IN AN ENTREPRENEURIAL EDUCATION MARKETPLACE

In a recent paper for the Thomas B. Fordham Institute, Hess argued that policy-makers in any domain have three main "quality-control" tools in their toolboxes: input and process regulation; outcome-based accountability; and market-based signals.

Input regulation entails policy-makers prescribing what entities must do to qualify as legitimate providers. Outcome-based accountability relies on setting performance targets that providers must meet. And market-based quality control permits the universe of users to choose their preferred providers—and then trusts that market pressures will reward good providers and eventually shutter lousy ones. [2]

Input and process regulation has been public education's primary quality-control strategy for one hundred years. We are all familiar with its hallmarks: requiring teachers to possess college degrees and licenses in the subjects they teach; requiring administrators to have advanced degrees and their own specialized licenses as well; mandating a prescribed number of hours or days of instructional time (overall and for particular subjects); setting limits on the number of students in each class; and so forth. These items—and more—are also the sorts of things that private accrediting bodies examine when doing their reviews.

Regulating inputs has certain advantages. It's a task well suited for large bureaucracies, which thrive on counting things and enforcing clear mandates without shades of gray. It's familiar. And it smacks of objectivity.

But there are real drawbacks too, as proponents of "reinventing government" and outcomes-based accountability have argued for at least twenty years. First, the relationship between inputs and results is tenuous. Teacher or administrator certification, for example, is hardly, if at all, linked to teacher or administrator effectiveness, making these poor proxies for quality. Second, these sorts of regulations constrain innovation and cost efficiency. What if a school can get the job done with 170 days of instruction instead of 180? What if uncertified teachers can get better results than certified ones? More broadly, what if on-the-ground educators think up myriad ways to build a better mousetrap, only to be snarled in red tape from the mousetrap central office?

Outcome-based accountability, then, has many desirable features. Educators can be held accountable for the ultimate aim of the education enterprise: more student learning. By focusing on the ends, it allows for all sorts of innovation around the means. And it's inspiring: it allows for the sort of professional autonomy that studies show most workers crave. But it has its imperfections too, as the No Child Left Behind era has demonstrated. As stated by Campbell's Law, holding people accountable for improving certain measures tends to warp behavior in unintended and often perverse ways. Teachers teach to the test, or cheat. Administrators narrow the curriculum. Energy is spent on the "bubble kids" right above or below proficiency cut scores, leaving low performers and high performers to fend for themselves.

Addressing these problems is difficult and expensive, and it carries additional risks. For example, one solution to the narrowing of the curriculum is to introduce testing in more subjects, but that only ramps up the time students spend preparing for and taking exams. Or policy-makers propose better tests—so teaching to them isn't such a crime—but balk at the additional expense.

What about market-based quality control? In many industries, "crowd-sourcing" websites like Trip Advisor gather the "wisdom of crowds" to provide quality-control feedback to potential consumers. Sites like Great Schools.org are attempting to bring this technology to education. Parents, with direct experience in schools, can offer a more comprehensive picture of a school's culture, approach, and environment than any set of standardized tests ever could. And assuming that parents care about more than a school's latest test scores—and much research indicates that they do—this could be a source of widely desired information.

Yet again, there are drawbacks. Crowd-sourcing sites can be gamed—in this case, by school administrators, who might post faux positive reviews. (It's not hard to imagine kids posting fake reviews, too.) Parents might not be discerning-enough consumers, loyal as they are to their chosen school. Alternatively, only disgruntled parents might take the time to post comments and feedback. Figuring out "quality control" for this quality-control metric is difficult in its own right.

So what's a quality-control hawk to do? Is all hope lost? As Hess argues, the best, if imperfect, approach is to use a smart combination of all three tools. Below we'll take a close look at how that could work in education's district-, charter-, and private-school sectors.

Which raises a key question: *Should* quality control work any differently in education's different sectors? Particularly when public funding is involved? Why not use the same tools for district, charter, and private schools?

The reason comes down to money: district and charter schools receive virtually all of their funding from public sources, and therefore public accountability should play a large role. (This is a version of the Golden Rule:

he who has the gold makes the rules.) Most private schools that participate in school voucher programs, however, receive relatively little public support, for most of their enrollment is made up of tuition-paying students. (The handful of private schools that do receive all or most of their funding via vouchers, on the other hand, should be treated essentially like public schools. More on that below.)

So the public has less of a right to demand certain outcomes for those schools writ large. And more importantly, if policy-makers attempt to exercise too much control of those private schools, the schools will simply refuse to participate in voucher programs, making them inoperative.

QUALITY CONTROL FOR PUBLIC SCHOOLS: DISTRICT AND CHARTER

Back to district and charter schools. Is there any reason to treat *them* differently from a quality-control perspective? Once upon a time, it was believed that charter schools deserved to be subject to less input regulation because they were subject to more outcome-based accountability: they could be shuttered if they didn't deliver on results. But two recent developments change the picture. First, we've learned that closing a low-performing charter school is incredibly difficult and happens rarely.[3] Second, federal and state policies have made the closure of district schools more feasible (if still challenging) than ever before. As a result, one could argue, outcome-based accountability is now virtually the same in both the district and charter sectors. And if minimal input regulations make sense for charter schools, why not extend that same approach to district schools?

So the ideal quality-control framework for public schools—both the district and charter variety—entails a handful of input/process regulations, a heavy dose of outcomes-based accountability, and the thoughtful use of market signals. And the framework is the same for both sectors.

Input Regulations for Public Schools

As explained above, the connection between most of public education's myriad input regulations and student achievement results is quite weak. In fact, in many cases these regulations impede achievement. Teacher- and principal-certification requirements, in particular, make it difficult to hire talented people from nontraditional backgrounds, such as candidates coming through Teach for America, New Leaders for New Schools, and other "alternative" programs, forcing them to return to school to attain paper credentials. Meanwhile, "seat time" mandates—that students spend 180 days, or 900 hours, per year in school—make the transition to high-quality online learning more difficult. If some students can prove "proficiency" in a shorter amount of time, why not let them?

The role of input regulations, then, should be minimal. But that doesn't mean it should be nonexistent. Some parts of "quality" will not be encouraged through outcome-based accountability and market signals alone. The role of input regulations, then, is to fill in the missing pieces. There are four main areas where it makes sense:

- *Health and safety.* Buildings should be designed properly; public-health measures should be enforced; criminal background checks should be mandatory for all adults working on school campuses.
- *Nondiscrimination.* Public schools should be expected to take all comers, except with carefully delineated exceptions. (For gifted-and-talented magnets, for example, or special schools for talented artists.) Public regulations should govern how schools select students when they are over capacity. (Lotteries are generally best, but allowances should also be made for schools that want to make extra efforts to recruit a diverse student body.) And public regulations will, no doubt, need to govern the treatment of students with disabilities.
- *Academic coverage.* Policy-makers should tread carefully here, but it's not unreasonable for the public to set some parameters around what a comprehensive school program must provide. (The public is paying the bills; it has some right to define what counts as a quality education.) Mandating that all students take history, science, physical education, art, and music, for instance, is appropriate. But such regulations should be crafted carefully to allow for local innovation. (For example, they shouldn't impede an inter-disciplinary approach.)
- *Financial propriety.* Regular audits should be mandatory; anti-nepotism rules should be enforced, and so forth.

Most notably, this recommendation means leaving many input regulations behind, including those governing:

- teacher and administration certification,
- seat time,
- class size,
- the use of technology, and
- the use of external contractors.

Outcomes-Based Accountability for Public Schools

If a "light touch" is ideal when it comes to input regulation, an aggressive approach is best when it comes to transparency and accountability around results.

This is hardly a new idea. For over a decade, the national policy community has debated the right measures and interventions as a part of the No Child Left Behind discussion. The advent of the Common Core State Standards, the significant federal funds available through the School Improvement Grants program, and new flexibility provided by the Obama Administration's ESEA waivers have reenergized the conversation.

A consensus is emerging, among reformers at least, that an appropriate transparency-and-accountability system contains five elements:

1. *Rigorous standards.* This one should be a no-brainer, but since the dawn of the standards-based reform movement in the 1990s it's been a surprisingly difficult hurdle to clear. Simply put, most state standards have been of very low quality: vague, voluminous, and not nearly ambitious enough. Thankfully, the Common Core State Standards, finalized in 2010 and adopted by forty-six states plus the District of Columbia, are clear, rigorous, and teachable.[4] Though limited to English language arts and math, they represent a significant step forward. Great standards are needed in the other major subjects too—science and history at the least.

2. *High-quality assessments.* This has been another disappointment: states have generally been unwilling to invest in state-of-the-art assessments, and they've also set "proficiency cut scores" at incredibly meager levels. The two federally funded assessment consortia that are developing tests linked to the Common Core have promised to change that; here's hoping they succeed.

3. *School report cards (and related data).* No Child Left Behind unleashed an avalanche of information, and mandated school-level report cards, with data disaggregated by myriad subgroups. Unfortunately, in most states these reports remain inscrutable to parents and the public. Thankfully, more states are starting to follow Florida's lead in giving schools easier-to-understand labels—often A through F grades—but much work remains to be done. (See more on this below under "market signals.")

4. *School inspectors.* This has not been a feature of most state accountability systems, but it's an idea whose time has come.[5] The notion is that even the best standards-testing and -reporting systems produce limited information; much nuance is lost when looking at numbers alone. School inspectors—hired by state education agencies or, in the

case of charter schools, authorizers—can get a closer on-the-ground look and provide reports to public agencies and to parents that go far beyond test scores. Using inspectors would help to mitigate the incentives to focus slavishly on state tests to the exclusion of all else.

5. *Thoughtful interventions.* Finally, robust accountability systems lead to action when schools are failing to measure up. This is the activity where reformers must be most humble, however, as efforts to date have been largely disappointing. Simply put, we don't know which interventions (particularly for chronically failing schools) are likeliest to result in real improvements, though the federal School Improvement Grants program may start to provide some hints. It's possible that in many cases, the only solution to a terrible school is a fresh start: shutting the school and starting over with new management and a new governance structure. But even that might not work. This is slightly more doable in the charter sector, where closure for low performance is supposed to be part and parcel of the model—but only slightly.[6]

Market-Based Signals for Public Schools

The third quality-control strategy is the appropriate use of market signals. In part, this means empowering parents with the information collected through a state's accountability system. State agencies and charter-school authorizers should develop user-friendly websites and school report cards; private entities like GreatSchools can provide information-packed portals for parents eager for even more data. (For more on provision and use of data, see Fullerton, this volume.)

But crowd-sourcing should be utilized, too. This is probably a role best played by the private sector, and it involves parents providing their own insights and impression about individual schools. Coupled with reports from professional school inspectors, this information could be powerful in shaping consumer behavior and in encouraging schools to be more responsive to their clients. Of course, that assumes that consumers have a choice, which is the responsibility of state and local policy-makers.

QUALITY CONTROL FOR PRIVATE SCHOOLS

As argued above, quality control will need to work differently for private schools receiving publicly financed vouchers—at least those enrolling just a handful of students. It's neither fair nor practical to expect such schools to submit themselves to the full panoply of process, outcomes, and market-based regulations. They simply will refuse to participate (especially if not allowed to use their regular admissions policies).[7]

What's needed, instead, is a "sliding scale" of accountability. This idea—first floated by the Fordham Institute three years ago—has recently been adopted in Louisiana.[8] In that state, schools that serve at least a minimum threshold of students are subject to a rating system akin to the accountability regime for public schools. Those that serve only a handful of scholarship students, on the other hand, are exempt. That's as it should be, for it balances the public's need for accountability with private schools' need for autonomy. Let's take a closer look.

Input Regulations for Private Schools

If loading up on input and process regulations makes little sense for district and charter schools, it makes even less sense for private schools. Here, states should tread very lightly and focus merely on health and safety (rules that private schools in most states already live by) and, as is the case in Milwaukee, financial propriety. The latter should be subject to the "sliding scale" concept too.

The small number of schools that serve just a handful of voucher students should be able to demonstrate that they spent the public funds on appropriate educational expenses. Schools that receive a great deal of public money, on the other hand, should continue to conduct annual independent audits, and those audits should be made more readily available to the public. Placing the audits on the Department of Public Instruction website, for example, is a logical step toward increased transparency.

These minimal regulations can be effective in weeding out shaky schools; in Milwaukee, more than forty private schools have become ineligible to participate in the choice program because of violations of its fiscal, health, and/or accreditation requirements.[9] And the School Choice Demonstration Project evaluation found that many of these schools were academically low-performing, too.[10]

Outcomes-Based Accountability for Private Schools

The issue of making public the academic achievement results of individual private schools has generated a great deal of controversy within the school-choice movement, but the momentum is clearly in the direction of greater transparency and accountability. The Milwaukee experience is instructive here. At the outset of the city's voucher program, schools were not required to publish test-score results. They certainly were not held accountable for them. But over time, additional testing and transparency requirements have been created, and the most recent evaluation of the program indicates that these measures might explain the recent improvements in voucher schools' results in Milwaukee.

As stated above, the country's most recently enacted voucher program, in Louisiana, has also embraced transparency and accountability for voucher schools—at least those serving a significant number of students. If Milwaukee's experience is any guide, this should result in a higher-quality program and better results. What makes sense for voucher schools, then, is the following:

1. *Quality controls on the front end.* As the Institute for the Transformation of Learning once did for Milwaukee, it makes sense for a respected entity or entities to screen new private schools' entry to voucher programs. The organizations currently approved to pre-accredit schools should be monitored based on the future success or failure of schools that they approved. Keeping the pre-accreditation screen strong can provide a quality-control check before new schools have the longevity—and money—to apply for accreditation.

2. *A sliding scale of transparency and accountability.* This would mean substantial public reporting for schools serving a large number of voucher students. The small number of schools serving just a handful of students, however, might be allowed to choose a nationally normed test and report only the results for the voucher students. This would remove a barrier to participation for new providers, especially those from newly eligible suburban private schools likely to take few students in their early years of participation. The large number of schools receiving virtually all of their funds from the public, on the other hand, should be subject to the state test, and results should be made public for all of their students. A recent study found that the overwhelming majority of private schools would not find such testing requirements objectionable.[11]

3. *Annual program-eligibility decisions.* States shouldn't have the authority to shut down low-performing private schools, but they can make them ineligible to receive public funds. To do this well, states will need to develop some sort of "authorizing" capacity, as in the charter sector. (More on this below.) Ideally, schools that are at risk of losing eligibility would be visited by school inspectors, and would also have access to an appeals process.

Market-Based Signals for Private Schools

As with district and charter schools, whatever information is collected about voucher-school performance should be made available on state websites and private ones, like GreatSchools. Crowd-sourcing strategies should be used for them, as well.

Charter Authorizing: A Model Worth Emulating in All Sectors

Perhaps the greatest innovation coming out of the charter-school sector isn't a particular instructional model or school design, but a new approach to school oversight: charter authorizing. The entities charged with holding charter schools accountable have spent twenty years perfecting an approach to quality control that moves away from the old system's command-and-control instincts and focuses instead on results.

In particular, a set of larger entities associated with the National Association of Charter School Authorizers—what one leader called Alpha Authorizers—has developed the tools and expertise to strike a better balance between input regulation and outcomes-based accountability. They obsess about getting quality right from the get-go—putting new-school applicants through an exhaustive screening process—and have clear processes for shutting down low-performing schools when all else has failed. But they also demonstrate the discipline not to micromanage their schools, allowing for the professional autonomy that is the key to the charter sector's energy and creativity.[12]

Several school districts are starting to pick up on these practices when it comes to their own traditional schools—especially districts such as Denver that are embracing the portfolio (or "diverse providers") model. (For more on the portfolio approach, see Horn and Evans, this volume.) A network of these districts, convened by the Center for Reinventing Public Education, is working to build the tools and expertise necessary to transform old-line central offices into organizations more akin to charter authorizers.[13]

The private-school sector could use entities like charter authorizers, too—organizations that would screen new private schools that want to participate in publicly funded voucher programs and could make them ineligible for such public funds if they fail to produce adequate results. In states that have introduced more public accountability into voucher programs—including Wisconsin, Indiana, and Louisiana—state education agencies are currently expected to play this role. Whether they have the right capacity or will to do so effectively remains to be seen, but it seems likely that separate organizations—authorizers for private schools—will need to be invented.

School Support Organizations

The quality-control framework sketched out above is more ambitious and comprehensive than any state has put in place so far. Still, it's incomplete without one more element: a serious effort to incubate high-quality schools. That's because even the most perfect policies aren't self-implementing. Getting laws, rules, and regulations right is important, but it's only the beginning. Cities that want to attract, replicate, and sustain high-quality schools need so much more; high-quality schools are unlikely to sprout from barren soil.

As Hess argued in his book *Education Unbound*, leaders need to pay attention to a community's school-reform ecosystem: public policies, yes, but also the web of funders, entrepreneurs, networks, and culture that makes it harder or easier for great schools to flourish. [14]

Perhaps the most concrete ingredient to put in place is an organization (or multiple organizations) that sees its job as making a city safe for new supply providers to flourish.

Models include New Schools for New Orleans, the New York City Center for Charter Excellence, and Indianapolis's Mind Trust. Some explicitly incubate high-quality schools, others recruit high-performing charter networks, and others provide direct services and professional development. But all were born from the insight that high-quality schools are unlikely to sprout out of nowhere; the ground must be groomed and seeded. (For more on this, see Kingsland, this volume.)

PUTTING THE QUALITY-CONTROL FRAMEWORK INTO ACTION

So what does this framework look like in a real place? Below is a rubric that cities can use to judge themselves against the ideal. We'll fill it in for Milwaukee—a city that proves our point that good policies aren't enough to guarantee high quality.

What should be clear from the table is that while Milwaukee has a few key quality-control pieces in place, much more remains to be done. Some of the action is at the state level: following through with stronger assessments and cut scores vis-à-vis the Common Core State Standards Initiative; making good on the promise to develop easier-to-understand school report cards; utilizing the Department of Public Instruction's new authority (under the Elementary and Secondary Education Act) to intervene in Milwaukee's worst public schools. Adding school inspectors to the mix would be a hugely positive—if cost-prohibitive—step.

But much can and should be done locally, too. Philanthropists and community leaders, in particular, can dramatically ramp up Milwaukee's quality-control system by:

- continuing to support GreatSchools' school-chooser guides and the organization's efforts to utilize "crowd-sourcing" much more extensively;
- helping to build the capacity of Milwaukee's charter-school authorizers, as well as entities in the private-school choice world that play a similar role (especially those empowered to prescreen new schools wanting to

Element	Score for Milwaukee				Comments
	Very Strong	Strong	Weak	Very Weak	
DISTRICT & CHARTER SCHOOLS					
<u>Outcomes-Based Accountability</u>					
Rigorous standards		X			Wisconsin took a big step forward when it replaced its own academic standards — among the worst in the nation — with the Common Core. Still, its standards in science and history are very weak.
High-quality assessments		X			Until recently, Wisconsin's "proficiency cut scores" were set at among the lowest in the nation, but the state recently raised the bar as part of its ESEA waiver application. The new Common Core assessments, if done well, should help, too.
School report cards				X	The Wisconsin Department of Public Instruction's entire website is inscrutable, not to mention its school report cards. A new and improved version is promised; the jury is out.
School inspectors				X	As is the case virtually everywhere in the U.S., school inspectors are not in use.
Thoughtful interventions			X		Neither Wisconsin nor Milwaukee Public Schools has been serious about closing low-performing schools, though they do have federal SIG money to do turnarounds. The state has the authority to intervene in the very worst schools under ESEA. A few charter authorizers have been willing to shutter failing charters.
<u>Market-based Signals</u>					
Crowd-sourcing site		X			Milwaukee is one of three cities in the country with a "School Chooser" guide published by GreatSchools.

Figure 2.1.   The Quality Control Framework, Applied to Milwaukee

participate in the voucher program); engaging the National Association of Charter School Authorizers to help on both fronts would be a smart move;
- launching a bona fide charter school (and private school) incubator for Milwaukee, modeled after New Schools for New Orleans or the Mind Trust's work in Indianapolis (for details on how to do this, see Kingsland, this volume);

PRIVATE SCHOOLS					
Outcomes-Based Accountability					
Screen on front end	X				Several entities are authorized by state law to play this role, including the Institute for the Transformation of Learning, Wisconsin North Central Association, and Wisconsin Religious and Independent Schools Accreditation.
Sliding scale		X			While there's no "sliding scale," transparency and accountability requirements have been increased. Schools must release test score results for voucher students.
Program eligibility				X	DPI does not have the authority to make schools ineligible due to poor performance.
Market-Based Signals					
Crowd-sourcing site	X				Private schools are included in the GreatSchools "School Chooser" Guide
School support			X		The Institute for the Transformation of Learning does some of this for charter schools, as does PAVE for private schools. MPS does not have much internal capacity on this front.

Figure 2.2. The Quality Control Framework, Applied to Milwaukee

- supporting the Milwaukee Public Schools' participation in the network of portfolio districts convened by the Center on Reinventing Public Education (Milwaukee is already a member);
- making fiscal information for choice, charter, and MPS schools readily available at a single digital location; and
- supporting the efforts of the Milwaukee Metropolitan Association of Commerce to produce a Milwaukee-specific school report card that includes information on private, public, and charter schools; efforts to improve the usefulness of this report card to parents and policy-makers should be ongoing.

CONCLUSION

Policy-makers, school choice advocates, community organizations, and reformers of every stripe have come to see quality control as job number one. By embracing the robust steps delineated herein, leaders in Milwaukee and nationwide can raise the game of their educational sectors. They should be careful, however, not to overdo it. We've tried command-and-control for one hundred years, and we know it doesn't work. For quality control to be something different—and something much more effective—designers need to control their own instincts to micromanage. Which city is ready to lead the way?

NOTES

1. Frederick M. Hess, *Revolution at the Margins* (Washington, DC: Brookings Institution Press, 2002), 7.

2. Frederick M. Hess, in *Education Reform for the Digital Era* (Washington, DC: Thomas B. Fordham Institute, 2012), 40.

3. David A. Stuit, *Are Bad Schools Immortal?: The Scarcity of Turnarounds and Shutdowns in Both Charter and District Sectors* (Washington, DC: Thomas B. Fordham Institute, 2010).

4. Sheila Byrd Carmichael, W. Stephen Wilson, Kathleen Porter-Magee, and Gabrielle Martino, *The State of State Standards—and the Common Core—in 2010* (Washington, DC: Thomas B. Fordham Institute, 2010).

5. Craig D. Jerald, "On Her Majesty's School Inspection Service," Education Sector, January 10, 2012, (accessed May 16, 2013).

6. Stuit, *Are Bad Schools Immortal?*

7. David A. Stuit and Sy Doan, *School Choice Regulations: Red Tape or Red Herring?* (Washington, DC: Thomas B. Fordham Institution, 2013).

8. Michael J. Petrilli, Chester E. Finn Jr., Christina Hentges, and Amber M. Winkler, *When Private Schools Take Public Dollars: What's the Place of Accountability in School Voucher Programs?* (Washington, DC: Thomas B. Fordham Institute, 2009).

9. Information provided to the author by Michael Ford, research director of the Wisconsin Policy Research Institute.

10. Brian Kisida, Laura I. Jensen, and Patrick J. Wolf, *The Milwaukee Parental Choice Program: Descriptive Report on Participating Schools 2009–2010*, SCDP Milwaukee Evaluation Report 27, March 2011.

11. Stuit and Doan, *School Choice Regulations*.

12. James N. Goenner, "Michigan's Chartering Strategy," *Education Next* 12, no. 3 (2012), http://educationnext.org/michigan%E2%80%99s-chartering-strategy (accessed September 14, 2012).

13. A list of the Portfolio School District Network members, as well as a description of the "7 Components of a Portfolio Strategy," are available at www.crpe.org/portfolio/districts.

14. Frederick M. Hess, *Education Unbound: The Promise and Practice of Greenfield Schooling* (Alexandria, VA: ASCD, 2010).

Chapter Three

The Recovery School District Model

Neerav Kingsland

THE TROUBLE WITH SCHOOL DISTRICTS

In most economic sectors in the United States monopolistic enterprises are either illegal, restricted, or tolerated out of necessity. The reasons we choose to avoid monopolies are multifold: monopolies reduce innovation, prevent choice, raise prices, and lead to lower productivity. Yet when it comes to our nation's most important endeavor—the education of our children—we grant near-monopolistic power to local school boards. These monopolies, while well-intentioned, reduce the opportunity for children to receive an excellent education. This is especially true in urban school districts.[1] If we expect to significantly change outcomes for students, we will need to change the system itself.

The specific negative effects of monopolistic governance on urban school districts can best be described as the governance trap. The governance trap looks like this:

> First, a "reform" school board is elected because everyone agrees the schools are failing children. Next, the school board hires a superintendent who agrees to come in and "fix" the system. Usually, the superintendent must tackle three main issues: improving dysfunctional labor relations, increasing the performance of recalcitrant bureaucracy, and managing a communications effort with a rightfully frustrated public. Inevitably, much political, financial, and emotional capital is spent. In most cases, minor improvements occur. In rare cases, modest improvements occur. Regardless, the progress is slow enough that a new "reform" school board is eventually elected, the previous superintendent is fired, and a new superintendent search begins. Repeat. Repeat. Repeat.

29

On average, this process of superintendent replacement takes over three and a half years—up from about two years and four months in 1999.[2] But more important than the length of the cycle are the results of the cycles. In part because of governance, our national student achievement is stagnating.

The governance trap is very real and very harmful to children. It is fueled by good intentions and antiquated structures, and it is sustained by the monopolistic nature of the system itself. Of all its harms, its greatest negative effects are on human capital and innovation. Labor relations decay to a level where great people avoid entering the system. And the lack of competition stunts innovation. The data bear this out: the United States now selects its teachers from the bottom third of college graduates and has significantly increased spending without much increase in productivity.[3]

RECOVERY SCHOOL DISTRICTS: A WAY OUT OF THE TRAP

Traditionally, reform-minded education leaders try to get out of the governance trap by utilizing one of three strategies: securing mayoral control, initiating a full state takeover, or electing a reform slate of school board candidates. The risk in each of these strategies is that one monopoly will simply replace another. Numerous major governance initiatives—mayoral control in Chicago and state takeover in Newark—have failed to deliver major changes. To achieve long-term governance improvements, monopolistic conditions must be reduced.

One promising vehicle for such a change is a Recovery School District, the first of which was created in Louisiana in 2003 and ushered in a wave of improved performance in New Orleans. Over the past six years, New Orleans has cut its achievement gap with the state by over 70 percent, and the percentage of students attending failing schools has been reduced from 78 percent to 40 percent. In large part because of the RSD, New Orleans has undergone one of the greatest educational turnarounds in our nation's recent history.

Leslie Jacobs, a prominent New Orleans business leader and member of the state board of elementary and secondary education, spearheaded the development of the nation's first RSD. Modeled after bankruptcy law, RSDs are charged with turning around failing schools. However, unlike traditional methods of reform, the RSD need not operate schools itself. It can utilize charter schools to overhaul individual schools as well as break up underperforming school systems.

In Louisiana, the RSD took over its first school in New Orleans in 2004, and the program expanded greatly after Hurricane Katrina. In New Orleans, this has led to the development of the nation's first major charter school district, with over 85 percent of students now attending charter schools. In recent years, two other states have created their own RSDs: the Achievement School District in Tennessee and the Education Achievement Authority in Michigan.

Structurally speaking, an RSD is a statewide school district that is charged with turning around a state's failing schools. It is generally situated within a state department of education and is led by its own superintendent, who usually reports directly to the state superintendent. Practically speaking, an RSD is a vehicle whereby a state can inject entrepreneurship, innovation, and new human capital into a stagnant and monopolistic local education system. An RSD is thus best understood as a bridge between a government monopoly and a liberalized educational system.

With three RSDs now in existence, the highest-value roles and functions of this new form of governance have become clearer. An RSD has the potential to transform a state's educational system by serving three primary functions:

- *Market creator.* An RSD can break local government monopolies by utilizing charter schools, alternative human-capital pipelines, and vouchers. In short, it can reduce both the school operation and the labor market share of a local monopoly. If well executed, this should lead to increased talent levels, innovation, and entrepreneurship in the system.
- *Ambassador and talent recruiter.* The RSD leader can be a legitimate ambassador for a new way of doing business. She can brand the RSD around academic excellence, recruit charter operators and human-capital providers, and be a leading voice for a state's most vulnerable children. The best RSD leaders are able to use their local and national networks to infuse the new system with the best educators in the nation. Market systems without great organizations and great people will provide limited results. A visionary RSD leader understands that people matter and that talent is a virtuous cycle. The best attract the best and so on.
- *Bankruptcy steward.* An RSD's legislative mandate is to turn around failing schools. However, unlike a typical takeover agency, the RSD's goal should not be to directly operate schools. Replacing one government monopoly with another is a fool's errand, and the history of district takeovers is dismal. Rather, the RSD's job should be more akin to that of a traditional banking regulator. If a bank fails, a banking regulator will intervene and either sell or rehab the institution, the key point being that the government does not operate the bank in perpetuity. It is a temporary steward, not a replacement operator.

RSDs can improve student achievement by acting as market creators, ambassadors, and bankruptcy stewards. Traditional school districts have been unable to separate educational governance from educational delivery, and charter schools continue to be either marginalized or viewed as a threat. Under an RSD governance model, charters can more fully flourish. Instead of being governed by their competitor (the district), charter schools can operate in an entrepreneurial zone where they become the primary deliverer of educational opportunity. A well-run RSD can correct the role of government in schooling and provide a way out of the governance trap—a trap that has plagued our nation's educational system for decades.

DESIGN PRINCIPLES: HOW TO CREATE AND LAUNCH A RECOVERY SCHOOL DISTRICT

Creating a high-performing RSD requires three major actions: getting the initial conditions right, hiring the right superintendent, and then overcoming the inherent and identifiable risks of decentralization.

Design Principle One: Getting the Prerequisites Right—Belief, Strategic Vision, and Policy Environment

Prerequisites for launching an RSD include holding a certain set of beliefs about education, molding these beliefs into a strategic vision, and developing a suitable policy environment:

- *Sharing a belief set.* An RSD will only achieve success if its creators (usually state governors, legislators, and policy-makers) believe that government officials must relinquish operational control of schools to educators and let parents choose which schools their children should attend. If this is not the case, at best the new government-run system will be marginally better than the previous. At worst, the new government leaders will create organizational chaos, most useful institutional knowledge of the old system will be lost, and schools will be reconstituted so haphazardly that performance will worsen. Beliefs matter and should be articulated at the outset.
- *Agreeing on a strategic vision.* Aligning on a set of beliefs is one thing. Translating these beliefs into a strategic vision is another. Case in point: leaders might all believe in educator empowerment, but they might be divided on whether this means autonomy within a governmental system or handing over full operational control to a nonprofit.

  In New Orleans, the RSD is now very clear on its strategic vision (after operating initially without such clarity). The RSD intends for every school it oversees to become a charter school. When necessary, it will directly operate schools for a limited amount of time. An RSD's strategy should be clear at the outset. It is impossible to build an aligned culture, organizational structure, and set of goals without strategic clarity. Most importantly, this strategy should embrace true autonomy in the form of third-party management of schools as the long-term goal.

- *Developing a suitable policy environment.* The right laws and policies are necessary but not sufficient. Specifically, the RSD itself will often require enabling legislation that allows for the creation of a subunit of the state to authorize charter schools. Additionally, an RSD's mandate should be clearly defined by a high-quality state accountability system.

For example, in Tennessee the RSD has jurisdiction over the bottom 5 percent of schools in the state. In many states, even such a narrow mandate will provide an initial jurisdiction of over a hundred schools, which could make for over a decade of work. While it may be tempting to expand the RSD's reach outside of failing schools, such work is best left to traditional statewide authorizers, which can complement RSDs by providing another route for charter-school expansion that is separate from failing-school replacement.

Additionally, all schools in the RSD must also be fully funded, with money following the child; operate outside of any local collective bargaining agreements; and have usage rights of government-owned facilities. Lastly, the RSD should be structured as an entity within the state department of education, and the RSD superintendent should report directly to the state superintendent.

In being managed by an education official rather than an elected board, the RSD superintendent will have more power to make difficult decisions in closing schools. Ideally, the governor and other state officials will also provide political support to the work of the RSD. (For example, in Louisiana, both Democratic and Republican governors have backed the RSD's expansion.)

Design Principle Two: Hiring a Humble, Connected, and Expert RSD Superintendent

The leader of a newly minted RSD inherits ideal conditions for a government educational post. There is no existing culture to be reformed, no existing strategies to be overhauled, and no unwieldy school system to be corralled. Rather, the RSD leader can build an institution, focus her energy on changing the management of a state's most underperforming schools, and slowly build a decentralized statewide school district that relinquishes power to educators and parents. But this opportunity will be realized only if the right person is at the helm. Some characteristics include:

- *A humble believer.* Very few superintendent candidates believe that the best way to improve student achievement is to let educators operate schools outside of direct governmental control. Most superintendents believe that the system can work if only someone like them is finally put in charge. In some sense, this is completely understandable; superintendents generally did not construct the systems they inherited.

But an RSD leader must not succumb to the temptation to improve schools through better direct operation. Rather, the RSD leader must humbly acknowledge that a marketplace of school operators will, over the long run, out-perform even the best direct-run system. In other words, the superintendent must relinquish power to educators rather than try to effect change through leadership alone.

- *A connector.* The ambassador function of an RSD leader should not be underestimated. Internally, the leader needs to build a high-quality management team. Externally, the RSD leader must recruit charter operators, human-capital providers, and school service providers. Hiring a leader who has worked in an entrepreneurial educational reform organization can pay many dividends. First, the RSD leader's professional and social network will be a key source of the first wave of talent. Second, reputation and accompanying trust go far across looser and more dispersed networks, which will be key to the success of the new system.
- *Knowledge of excellent schools.* Lastly, an RSD leader should understand how excellent schools are run, either through experience operating a high-performing school or working for an institution that partnered closely with such schools. Her internal bar must be high. A leader who does not understand what great schools look like, feel like, and perform like will be at risk of making flawed decisions at every turn. At the end of the day, the RSD leader sets the bar for the new system, and if this bar is low, it may cap the long-term performance of the system.

Design Principle Three: Preparing for and Mitigating the Major Risks of Decentralization

Developing an RSD comes with serious risks. In Louisiana, the RSD expanded ahead of its abilities to attract qualified senior staff and build organizational structures. Its early results in operating schools were weak, which led to poor initial student outcomes. Moreover, the RSD did not fully assume its proper role as sound regulator until years into its existence. Some of these mistakes were avoidable. Others were driven by the necessities of operating in the wake of one of the worst natural disasters in our nation's history.

The risks of launching an RSD mirror those of most decentralization and deregulation efforts. Across sectors, risks include:

- *Oligarchy formation.* A government monopoly may simply be replaced with a private monopoly or oligarchy (e.g., natural resources in Russia post-communism).
- *Regulatory capture.* Government regulators may be "captured" by the new elite. The banking industry's inability to be regulated serves as caution.
- *Lack of fortitude.* Lastly, sometimes things get worse before they get better (e.g., Eastern European economies after the breakup of the Soviet Union). Knowing when to pull the plug and when to persevere can be exceedingly difficult.

For RSDs specifically, key risks include:

- *Poor regulation, passive oversight.* Lax charter authorization, weak accountability systems, and poor oversight will lead to mediocre student achievement outcomes and severe equity issues. The RSD must take its regulatory responsibilities seriously. In Louisiana, the RSD utilizes the National Association of Charter School Authorizers to make recommendations on approving or rejecting charter applicants. Additionally, the RSD has developed "Equity Reports" on every school in the city to provide transparency and oversight on issues such as student retention, expulsion, and special education. Most recently, the RSD instituted a centralized enrollment system in New Orleans to ensure that all parents had equal access to schools across the city.

  The RSD cannot be a passive regulatory agency It must determine when system-level issues trump what should generally be an extreme deference toward school autonomy.
- *Going too slow, going too fast.* Creating markets is hard work. Policy development, human-capital formation, and new organization incubation all take significant time and resource investments. As in democracy formation, an initial set of laws only goes so far. While there is no set formula for the pace of liberalization, a tentative pacing of moving 5 percent of schools each year from traditional district public into the charter or voucher sector seems to be a fairly useful rule of thumb. But local conditions will dictate how fast the decentralization efforts can be responsibly executed. Going too fast will lead to poor quality. Going too slow will cause unnecessary harm to students by keeping them trapped in underperforming schools.
- *Building the right team.* The right senior leadership in the early years of an RSD is crucial. This initial team will exert heavy influence on who opens schools, which schools are closed, and the content of the new policy regime. Additionally, the team will need to build constructive relationships with charter operators—and these relationships will affect the long-

term growth trajectory of operator expansion (who will choose to expand elsewhere to the extent the RSD is mismanaged).

Superintendents who do not spend significant time and resources on building a management team will soon mirror the underperforming bureaucracies that the RSD is meant to improve. In some sense, the RSD itself is another government monopoly. As such, much care must be exercised in building the team and culture at the outset. Specifically, attracting the right blend of entrepreneurial, educational, and management expertise is essential. Traditional district officials may not thrive in this new setting.

ACTION STEPS

The section below details specific action steps that Wisconsin could take to create an RSD. However, the general actions and principles could apply in a variety of different state contexts.

Enacting Legislation

The Walker recall makes clear that education reform in Wisconsin is a divisive issue. A coalition of willing legislators may be difficult to come by. However, RSDs have now been created in both blue states (Michigan) and red states (Louisiana and Tennessee). And the idea of replacing failing schools with charter schools is also supported by both parties. Suggestions for building a coalition include:

- *Align actors around a common vision.* In Tennessee this was turning around the bottom 5 percent of schools in the state. In Wisconsin, it will be important to align a coalition that includes the governor, state superintendent, Metropolitan Milwaukee Association of Commerce, and, ideally, legislators who represent the Milwaukee area.
- *Take learning visits.* Bring education and political leaders to Louisiana to see firsthand the positive effects of an RSD. Include schools led by both new and veteran leaders so as to clearly demonstrate that all educators can flourish under autonomous conditions. Numerous city and state leaders have visited New Orleans and had their beliefs changed by talking to educators on the ground. This is especially true of those leaders who may view charter schools as a type of corporate reform that is meant to undermine public education.
- *Connect to the state accountability system.* Ensure that a statewide accountability system clearly articulates how and when the RSD entity can intervene. Louisiana, Tennessee, and Michigan all define RSD jurisdiction in different manners. Develop rules that set up the RSD for manageable

and continual impact. Utilizing growth measures in the state accountability system will also go far in ensuring that the RSD is both turning around the most underperforming schools and being rewarded for the gains it makes with struggling schools.

- *Utilize foundation support.* Numerous national foundations have come out in support of RSD-type entities, and local foundations often have significant influence over the political and business community. Securing philanthropic support can allow the RSD to staff ahead of growth, ensuring that people and processes are in place to support expansion.

Additionally, to the extent that philanthropy is available to support charter expansion and human-capital development (rather than less impactful educational programs), the RSD will be better able to move quickly in its pursuit of creating new, high-quality options for students. Specifically, local citywide intermediaries can be useful in coordinating philanthropy to support entrepreneurial reforms. In New Orleans, Tennessee, and Detroit, these organizations have accelerated local reforms.

Recruit an Exceptional Superintendent

The first superintendent will greatly influence the future success of the RSD. Some suggestions for recruiting and selecting an excellent superintendent include:

- *Do not make selection a public process.* Stakeholder input is best solicited at the criteria stage of selection. Once recruitment begins, the best candidates will not want to participate in an elongated public trial. Selection should be driven by the state superintendent and her network.
- *Hire a reform-connected search firm.* Two to three prominent search firms dominate the education reform market; hire one of them to manage the process. Then work very closely with the search firm in surfacing, cultivating, and selecting candidates. Ultimately, the new superintendent will work for the state and not for the search firm, meaning that state leaders must be present and proactive in recruitment. The energy devoted to this search should rival the energy spent by state leaders in recruiting private-sector companies to do business in the state.
- *Have patience.* Launching with the right RSD leaders is worth waiting for. If necessary, move implementation back one year to find the right candidate, because a poor first year of implementation can greatly reduce long-term effectiveness.
- *Select a network.* Understand the candidates' networks, and select a candidate whose network will deliver additional resources. Leaders coming out of the entrepreneurial education sector will often have significant ties to high-performing charter and human-capital organizations.

- *Filter for strategy.* Ensure that the candidate actually believes that relinquishing power to educators is a better reform strategy than improving government-operated schools. *Autonomy* means different things to different leaders. Do not assume that leaders coming out of the entrepreneurial sector will necessary hold these beliefs. Currently, the reform community is not unified around the strategy of delegating operation of schools to nongovernmental entities.

Launch Thoughtfully

Launching an RSD is difficult, and there are only a few models to follow. Here are some suggestions:

- *Align strategy, structure, and people.* Build the organization for what it will execute. Review organizational charts from other RSDs to understand how to structure the organization, and then hire for alignment and potential rather than district experience. Do not build an organization that is meant to directly operate schools. Build an organization that can act as an ambassador and accountability agent.
- *Resist emergency calls for more.* The experiences of RSDs across states all point toward extreme pressures on quick growth. Governors and state superintendents will want results quickly and demand full district turnaround. Ignore them. Tackle urban markets with 5 to 10 percent annual growth targets. In Milwaukee, this would mean launching six to twelve schools a year at the outset and increasing this rate as the market matures. Achieving measurable success in the first three to five years will create the conditions necessary to execute the second wave of work.
- *Secure anchor tenants.* In the first year of existence, get at least one or two exceptional charter operators to commit to significant growth. Examples of excellence are crucial, and early wins will buttress inevitable failures. High-performing charters will raise the bar for all operators, as well as groom future leadership. Talent cycles are virtuous, and having organizations that grow leaders will lead to the growth of more high-performing charter operators down the road.
- *Emphasize recruitment over development.* In failing environments, school improvement plans and increased professional development are siren songs that will lead to marginal improvements. Focus on getting the right people on board before relying on improvement strategies. Years in, development will yield better results, but not at the outset.
- *Close 100 percent of schools that do not meet performance targets.* The early years of accountability will affect both the long-term structure and the culture of the new system. The RSD must close or transform all schools in its portfolio that do not meet performance targets—even if these

schools are marginally better than what exited before. Early exceptions to accountability rules will undermine the integrity of the system.

Hold the Mirror Up Often

Education reformers have a tendency to view their work in the best possible light. Most superintendents feel that they are on track for dramatic gains. Historical evidence demonstrates that most of them will be wrong. Some suggestions for continually increasing performance:

- *Hire an evaluator.* Set specific goals, and have an external evaluator measure your progress against these goals. The best researchers will be brutally honest. They can also provide statistical evidence that surpasses most state accountability systems (utilizing experimental and quasi-experimental studies).
- *Benchmark yourself.* Have a clear understanding of how other recovery districts have performed, and track the new district against these metrics. School quality, market share, and human-capital recruitment are all worth tracking.
- *Respond to what you see.* It will be tempting to dismiss information contrary to perceived realities. Force yourself to correct course. Accelerate or slow depending on your performance. If necessary, focus on charter replacement rather than charter market-share growth, with the goal of expanding the charter sector only if it is out-performing the traditional sector.
- *Allow time.* Be humble and responsive but know that markets take time to build. Comprehensive results may take years, although a complete void of early successes should be cause for pause.

CONCLUSION

Governance is only one piece of the puzzle in raising student achievement across our country. But it is an essential piece, as it is only through governance that educator autonomy and parent empowerment can be achieved. Our antiquated governance structures are not fit to spur on the innovation necessary to increase the effectiveness of our schools. Yet, given our current power structures, government itself must initiate this transition to relinquish control back to educators and parents. RSDs are among the most powerful tools available to bring about this change.

NOTES

1. Herbert J. Walberg and Joseph L. Bast, *Education and Capitalism: How Overcoming Our Fear of Markets and Economics Can Improve America's Schools* (Stanford, CA: Hoover Institution Press, 2003).

2. Council of Great City Schools, "Urban School Superintendents: Characteristics, Tenure, and Salary," *Urban Indicator,* Fall 2010, www.cgcs.org/cms/lib/DC00001581/Centricity/Domain/4/Supt_Survey2010.pdf (accessed September 14, 2012).

3. Byron Auguste, Paul Kihn, and Matt Miller, *Closing the Talent Gap: Attracting and Retaining Top Third Graduates to a Career in Teaching* (New York: McKinsey & Company, 2010); James Guthrie and Elizabeth A. Ettema, "Public Schools and Money," *Education Next* 12, no. 4 (2012), http://educationnext.org/public-schools-and-money (accessed September 14, 2012).

Chapter Four

From "Professional Development" to "Practice"

Getting Better at Getting Better

Doug Lemov

Ultimately, every school is the same in one critical way. Rural, suburban, or urban; private, public, or charter; high-performing, average, or in crisis, every school allocates about 75 to 80 percent of its resources to staff salaries and benefits. In the end, a school buys people's time, effort, and expertise and, you could argue, not much else. Every school is a collection of people with the shell of a building around it.

The implications of this simple observation are significant. To improve an organization consisting almost entirely of people and predicated on their skill and capacity, managing and maximizing human capital is the highest leverage tool for improvement.

Generally, the strategies that schools and school systems use to manage human capital fall into three categories:

- *Labor market strategies* wherein a school or school system attempts to attract and retain better people.
- *Incentive strategies* wherein a school or school system attempts to use incentives and accountability systems to make people perform better.
- *Development strategies* wherein a school or school system attempts to use training and professional development to increase the aggregate skill level of its employees.

For the most part, school improvement efforts have focused on the first two categories. The advent of new and better—if also more controversial—teach-

41

er evaluation systems is perhaps the single most dominant discussion in this arena today. The role and fate of teachers at the bottom, and sometimes the top, of the "growth tables" that are produced by many of these evaluation systems are sources of vociferous public debate. Focus on these two aspects of human capital is not without merit. Improving who works in our schools and how they are incentivized to act are important factors. But they are at best incomplete without an intense focus on the third category, being more effective at making people better.

Endeavors in the development category are often especially challenging, which may explain why they are less prevalent in the current conversation about improving schools. Development strategies must overcome an established historical precedent of low-quality professional-development offerings and resulting teacher skepticism. They must win over teachers who are often suspicious when asked or required to attend development sessions. ("I must be here because people question my work.")

Plus there's the plain fact that we continue to have limited insight into what works—either in the classroom or in the training sessions—and how to support teachers in applying what they've learned in the training sessions to their classrooms. As a result, professional development often becomes an afterthought, with insufficient investment or consideration resulting in ineffective approaches. Thus, the most powerful management tools go unused and remain underleveraged.

This paper describes the value of better development strategies and presents case studies to illustrate the route to more effective professional development—training that makes schools better at making teachers better. These strategies might address some of the challenges faced by Milwaukee Public Schools, which, for just over 4,600 FTE teachers,[1] spent more than $3 million on "districtwide professional development," and more than $5 million on what the budget identifies as "teacher quality" programs, including the mentor teacher program and the Milwaukee Teacher Education Center, in FY 2011.[2]

But this chapter will also assume that many of those challenges are typical and endemic to the field. In particular it will describe how a schoolwide commitment to *practice* in teacher development might improve teacher performance in a broad range of areas; build a positive school culture marked by collegiality, humility, and high rates of satisfaction; and help make incentive systems more productive, resulting in higher rates of teacher retention.

In short, though it is humble and may seem unspectacular at first, designing improved teacher training around the idea of *practice* has the capacity to "shift the curve," improving teacher quality dramatically and relatively quickly across the board. Further, incentive and labor market strategies are only truly effective when combined with robust development strategies. Invigorated by a commitment to making teachers at every phase of their careers a little better every week, application of all three categories of human-capital management can have a dramatic effect on results—and applied in this manner are more likely to result in teacher satisfaction as well.

But before examining further, it's worth taking a moment to define a key term. In using the word *practice*, I am referring to the word in a limited and (to some) mundane sense. *Practice* is a time when colleagues meet together and participate in exercises that encode core skills. That is, the thing you would see a basketball team or an orchestra do as a matter of course but that teachers are rarely asked to do and rarely consider. Among teachers, it might involve teaching parts of their lessons to one another, revising lesson plans in groups, or even role-playing interactions with disruptive students. In fact, several high-performing school systems, from those in Japan to some of the most successful charter networks in the United States, routinely approach training in this manner with outstanding results.

SYNERGY BETWEEN DEVELOPMENT STRATEGIES AND OTHER APPROACHES TO HUMAN-CAPITAL MANAGEMENT

While it certainly makes sense to try to attract and retain the best teachers possible, as a profession, teaching can't wait for the large-scale macroeconomic changes that might or might not attract a broader and deeper pool of candidates to the field. Organizations in the sector must begin improving immediately and so must be prepared to succeed with the current labor pool. Further, effectively developing people—making them successful at their work—not only is a key aspect of a healthy teacher-retention strategy but also, as recent research by TNTP[3] found, may be most effective at retaining the most valuable teachers. On the other hand, while incentive strategies— value-added assessments, performance-based pay—are all important, they hold imminently less leverage if teachers don't know what to do to "win" or if schools leave them to sink or swim.[4]

Finally it's worth noting that from a public-policy perspective, there is even greater incentive to invest in developmental strategies than at the individual school (or school system) level. A single school can succeed by attracting better teachers or getting better at motivating those already in the system, but, seen more broadly, such victories are pyrrhic.

Consider an individual school that "successfully" recruits four or five outstanding teachers. The school improves, and 150 students in the classrooms with the new teachers receive a better education, but at the cost to 150 students in other schools who have lost their outstanding teachers. Strategies that do not develop the overall level of teacher skill merely determine who gets access to the scarce and precious resource of high-quality teaching. Without a commitment to increasing skill, it is a zero-sum game, and if that remains the case, individual schools can win, but the sector as a whole will run short of talented teachers and inevitably lose.

In the end, then, increasing the quality of currently employed teachers through training is not only deeply synergistic with other human-capital reforms (it helps guide teachers to navigate incentives successfully and helps retain top performers) but also the most sustainable. Good training has the benefit of being relatively cheap and easily scaled and differentiated. Everyone can be trained and made better no matter where they are on the growth curve.

BETTER, YES! BUT HOW?

Ironically, given their mission of fostering the acquisition of knowledge and skills in students, schools have historically been poor at developing knowledge and skills among the adults who work for them, in part because they often have little sense for what helps their students succeed. These two core problems of schools are directly linked: schools fail to help students succeed because they fail to make teachers better, and they fail to make teachers better because they do not spend enough time studying the things that successful teachers do. Any lasting improvement in teacher development, then, must begin with a clearer commitment to understanding what works.

This is a more promising and more local proposition than it might seem. Today's educators live amidst a historic flowering of data, even compared to educators a few years ago. Ten years ago, few, if any, schools had reliable data on most of their teachers. If they did, the data were rarely in a form that made them comparable to data about a large enough pool of other teachers to put them in context and say, for example, "This teacher is outstanding."

Five years ago, schools began to have this sort of information but still lacked basic statistical analytic tools such as regressions and value-added analyses to allow them to filter out significant sources of "noise"—student socioeconomic status, for example—that clouded their data. Now, however, possibly for the first time, a school has the capacity to look at itself and other schools, should it choose, and reasonably hope to answer questions such as:

- Who are our best teachers?
- What do they do that makes them different from the rest?
- What specific strengths and understandings do we have within our organization?
- How can we leverage those things to make ourselves better?

The Milwaukee Public Schools, for example, have worked with the Value-Added Research Center at the Wisconsin Center for Education Research to produce school-level data for some time. The district releases high-quality information for accountability purposes. However, it also presents an untapped opportunity to use that data internally to better understand and leverage the district's successes. Similar high-quality data are available to Milwaukee's charter and choice sectors but also present an untapped opportunity in the area of professional development. In fact, the data represent an ideal opportunity for the district and choice sectors to collaborate and mutually benefit.

The notion that informing teacher development goals can be, at least in large part, a local task contradicts the traditional approach that has tended to assume that expertise comes from centralized sources like universities, district offices, and publishers. But such guidance was inherently far removed from the day-to-day work of teachers. At best, it was useful but not adapted to or informed by local conditions. At worst, it was based on ideological goals rather than measurable improvements in student learning—"this is what good teaching should be" versus "this is what good teaching *is*." Almost assuredly it sent the message that expertise lay elsewhere.

Effective teacher development often starts, then, with the idea of organizational self-reflection and reflection focused as much on what works as on what does not work. A better approach to teacher development starts with the assumption that the solutions to teaching problems exist in the classrooms of practicing teachers. Such an approach not only begins the process with a vote of confidence in teachers but also builds a positive culture that says, "We are doing things well. We're going to honor our successful methods and teachers by studying them." This shift to a positive message implicit in training is critical. In a culture where teachers worry about being "blamed" for bad schools, they now become the solution.

Studying what works—even at the local level—is also a key starting point for professional development because it increases the likelihood that training will focus on what is germane, practical, and effective. This is critical in light of the fact that school systems continue to make large investments in helping teachers improve their knowledge and skills, generally with little effect.

A recent policy brief by the Consortium for Policy Research in Education estimated that between 3 and 6 percent of total school spending was allocated to professional development.[5] This means that roughly $20 billion to $30 billion per year is spent on professional development with questionable results, at best. The policy brief notes:

> Teachers typically spend a few hours listening and, at best, leave with some practical tips or some useful materials. There is seldom any follow-up to the experience and subsequent in-services may address entirely different sets of topics. . . . On the whole, most researchers agree that local professional devel-

opment programs typically have weak effects on practice because they lack
focus, intensity, follow-up and continuity.

In other words, what we do to train teachers routinely fails to make them
better teachers. As one teacher in Milwaukee put it, "They put together
things that they think we want or need, but the things we really need we do
not get." "I hate to say it," said another, "it's almost a waste of time."

WHAT DOES INEFFECTIVE LOOK LIKE?

While no single factor explains why professional development is generally of
such low quality, the factors that commonly contribute to poor outcomes
include:

- *Training that is organizationally disconnected.* Teacher training that is
  disconnected from the school's culture and management often features
  outside "experts" rather than internal leaders presenting material and/or it
  is rarely connected directly to evaluation, observation, or other follow-up.
  A workshop on questioning is rarely followed up by school leaders making observation rounds to "see how it's going" and share successes across
  the school. Further, there is rarely a second workshop on the topic in
  which teachers present and discuss challenges and successes from their
  efforts to implement the ideas and strategies. Teachers who attend sessions are presented with little reason or expectation that they will put the
  ideas into practice with diligence or that they will even try them at all.
- *Training that is "one and done."* Topics tend to come up once, often at
  infrequent meetings or workshops, to be "covered" and not addressed
  again. Most effective teachers recognize that complex material requires
  multiple exposures before students master them. Mastery of multiplying
  fractions requires introduction one day, review the next, practice for two
  or three more, assessment, and then further review if necessary. There is
  no reason to think that learning to teach would be any different.

  That said, few schools appear to return to training goals repeatedly,
  working on a teaching skill multiple times and allowing teachers to practice it until the point of mastery. Time allocated to training at most schools
  is limited; therefore, it is additionally critical that schools train teachers
  on the most important things to ensure their success. There is no sense
  conducting a workshop on gender equity in questioning if the behavioral
  environment prevents teachers from asking questions effectively. Training
  on topics of peripheral importance to teaching or on topics that are not
  about teaching at all is a common distraction.
- *Training that marginalizes the role of practicing teachers.* As described
  above, professional development in many schools and districts conceives

of teachers as being primarily the recipients of training, rather than shapers and designers of it. Training is done more "at" teachers than it is "by" teachers.

* *Training that values thinking over doing.* Most district training focuses on thought: how to think about the questions you ask, your relationships to children, the content you teach. They are essentially presentation format. No math teacher would hope for mastery based on even the finest presentation without asking students to complete multiple sets of problems—to practice executing the skill in different settings and with different challenges at different levels of difficulty. As I will discuss below, this challenge is endemic to professional development and perhaps the most damning of all.

This broader picture is borne out in Milwaukee, where teachers describe an approach to professional development that is counterproductive; it fails to make them better but succeeds in adding to their frustrations. In a recent focus group conducted to hear the opinions of professionals, a group of teachers was asked about the professional development they receive:

Teacher 5: Occasionally we have . . . built-in time off, and you will be told to go to a particular school, or you may have something at your particular school, somebody coming in and doing workshops on particular things, but that's the extent—

Interviewer: Is it helpful when it happens?

Teacher 4: No.

Teacher 1: No.

Teacher 4: It's very ineffective, if you ask me. . . . It's just a big, huge room, a bunch of teachers in a room, one person up there trying to talk, and sometimes it's nothing to do with nothing, talking about the reading that day. I hate to say it, it's almost a waste of time; I'd rather be working in the classroom.

Teacher 1: I think they're out of touch. When you have people at central office, they're away from children, and they put together things that they think we want or we need, but the things we really need are things we don't get. Everything is scripted. You give us lectures and it's scripted. It has nothing to do with the price of tea in China. It's worthless, it—you could have sent this to me in an email, saved your money, because it's ineffective.

The following two case studies examine how schools in the charter-school sector have chosen to engage in professional training differently. Though both professional-development cases were highly effective in supporting each school's successful academic results, there is nothing inherently "charter" about the approaches they have employed, nothing that district schools somewhere have not also done successfully and nothing a district school could not replicate if it chose to.

CASE STUDY 1: INCREASING THE RATIO OF STUDENT DISCUSSIONS

Consider the development of Molly, a successful reading teacher at Troy Prep Middle School, a charter school in upstate New York. In her fourth year of teaching, Molly had good evaluations. Her classroom was not perfect— she and her principal had identified several important areas where they agreed she should strive to improve. But her results significantly exceeded the scores of most sixth-grade reading teachers in her district, and, even with more than 90 percent of students in Molly's school living in poverty, they also exceeded those of many teachers in more prosperous suburban districts.

Molly worked hard, and her principal noted that she showed a keen interest in improvement. She had suggested most of the professional goals in her evaluation. In this way, she was fairly typical of teachers who are failed by professional development within their schools. Teachers are most likely to get support around classroom practices if they are new to the profession or if they are struggling, but Molly was neither: she was quietly capable, good but not yet great.

Oftentimes schools and even teachers themselves assume that good teachers do not need improvement and development, but this is not the case. Molly had survived the first three years of urban teaching, and this alone makes her important. By some estimates more than 50 percent of urban teachers leave the profession in the first five years.[6] Molly was about to pass the early high-turnover years, which means she was an especially critical person in whom to invest. She had the capacity and willingness to improve, and improvements in her practice were likely to play out over a career longer than a year or two. Compared to investing in a shaky novice who was likely to crash out of the profession, the expected value of making Molly better was raised by the prospect of a long career in teaching.

Molly attended a professional-development session run by her principal and several lead teachers in her school. The training focused on increasing "ratio," the amount of cognitive work students do in the classroom compared to the amount of cognitive work teachers do in the classroom. The training asked teachers to bring in a lesson plan they intended to teach in the next week and to draft and revise specific questions to ensure that they pushed cognitive work onto students. The session was practical and helpful, and Molly got useful feedback on her questions. However, when she taught the lessons the following week, she found herself faced with a common and age-old problem. The questions she asked in response to the novel her class was reading were better, but the answers students gave were often unexpected, and Molly found herself unsure of how to respond on multiple occasions. When this happened, Molly would often end the discussion by providing the answer herself, and students became disengaged.

Even though the training had been positive, Molly did not see an immediate difference, and she began to worry. However, her principal quickly followed up on the workshop and by Wednesday of the next week had stopped by Molly's class and checked in on her via e-mail. Molly acknowledged that the training had not changed much in her class, so the principal asked Molly to contact Ella, a colleague whose results had identified her as a top-performing reading teacher and who, his observations confirmed, was especially effective in leading discussions.

Ella suggested that Molly meet with her for ten minutes three or four mornings a week and simply practice handling the situation. Every morning for four weeks, Molly would read questions from her lesson plan to Ella, Ella would give a typical wrong student answer, and Molly would practice responding to the unexpected answer. Sometimes Ella would give Molly advice and Molly would re-ask the question and practice responding in a different way. Sometimes Molly would hear something she herself didn't like and self-correct. Sometimes they brainstormed possible responses together until they found something that seemed right.

Over time Molly got better at responding to unexpected wrong answers. She was able to keep the discussion going and let students participate more. She became confident, poised, and able to think on her feet. Discussions in her classroom began to flower and her ratio improved. And because responding to the challenging situations became intuitive to her, they required less of her processing capacity. Her mind could be on other things—what her next question should be, which students might be disengaged in the lesson—even while she handled the situations better.

Further Molly came to believe that dramatic changes in her own skill were well within her grasp. She could identify something she wanted to get better at, practice with a peer, and, in a few short weeks, be altogether better at her life's work. Molly's success was dramatic enough that the school used staff meetings to replicate the practice activity Molly and Ella had developed. Teachers would meet in small groups and practice responding to student answers. Over time, the school's teachers began to recognize further areas in which they could improve their skills through practice. A culture of regular practice among the staff developed, and the school, despite a poverty rate above 90 percent, has rapidly become one of the top-performing schools in the state.

The training at Molly's school was different from typical teacher professional development in several key ways. Most significantly, it relied on two very unusual sources for solutions to problems in the classroom. First it relied on teacher knowledge to uncover good solutions to classroom challenges. It tapped a "local" expert in Ella, who, because she worked in the same school, had credibility with Molly and was able to build an ongoing relationship. But the training also tapped Molly's own knowledge—she and Ella brainstormed and analyzed solutions together. In that way, it expressed faith in the professionalism of both teachers (and later the whole staff) to uncover solutions.

The training was also different in that it spiraled. First, the sessions with Ella were initiated by the principal's follow-up after a workshop and the open and honest conversation he and Molly had about her struggle to improve. When she struggled, they stayed on the topic. Then, the sessions with Ella were cyclical too. Molly and Ella met regularly. They corresponded by e-mail to process how actual classes were going. They observed each other.

Their process recognized that mastery was not going to be achieved in a single afternoon. Interestingly, the training also helped Ella, who reported benefiting from the practice herself. And the success of the training on a small scale was quickly replicated across the school, allowing the entire staff to share insights about increasing ratio.

Perhaps the most important difference between the training Molly received and typical professional development, however, was the emphasis on practice. The training didn't stop when an effective strategy (e.g., "When you hear a wrong answer, ask another question that causes students to understand what's wrong about the thinking.") was identified. Ideas are easy, but execution is hard, so Molly and Ella continued working well beyond the point where Molly could reliably identify a good response to an answer. They practiced until Molly could implement it on the spot with fluidity and poise, until she could respond to a wide variety of answers, until she could do it smoothly enough that she could attend to everything else in her class while deploying the skill.

Practice Prepares for Performance

Several aspects of Molly's professional-development success made it distinctive, but the one that Molly thought made the difference is the one that is arguably most unusual in the profession—the inclusion of regular rounds of practice at simple drills that prepared Molly for the classroom. In all, Molly practiced responding to perhaps a hundred examples of wrong answers before she began to execute effectively during her teaching.

Though it is rarely referred to as such, teaching is a performance profession. It happens live, and an outstanding lesson on Tuesday guarantees little about Wednesday's outcome. You have to perform all over again. If Wednesday's lesson is undone by unexpected student misconceptions or distractions, a teacher cannot stop and call a colleague to guide her through the tricky parts, as a lawyer or a writer might do. She or he is "on stage," performing live in front of thirty or so students.

Every other performance profession—athletics, the arts, surgery—prepares for the dynamics of their work via practice. In fact they don't call what they do to prepare for a performance "professional development." They call it practice, and their goal is to rehearse the moves they will require in the game or on stage dozens if not hundreds of times before they play for keeps. A tennis player wouldn't dare step onto center court at Wimbledon to try out a new backhand; she would have practiced it over and over in a series of training sessions. Similarly, a surgeon would practice his suturing over and over before putting needle to live tissue.

Performance professions understand that you get good at what you do in the game by practicing it beforehand, that practice reduces stress during performance and frees your mind to be more responsive to situations that develop during performance. And in most cases, practice turns out to be a time for team-building and developing collegiality. Practicing together makes a team sport out of an endeavor that might otherwise be marked by isolation. Peers who practice together expose their weaknesses, share solutions, and reflect on the goals they hold in common. They rely on one another for solutions and camaraderie. This makes them feel like a part of something.

Practice can develop both skill and capacity among all performers and *especially* those who, like Molly, are already strong, while also fostering morale and team spirit. Practice sessions at Molly's school were upbeat and characterized by laughter and hard work. Teachers worked with a partner for ten minutes and then switched and worked with someone else. They reported feeling relieved to be able to work through the challenges of their day with a colleague who understood. They soon began practicing how to handle difficult behavioral interactions and complex instructional moments. They even practiced lesson planning, which you can read more about below.

CASE STUDY 2: LESSON STUDY

Like Molly and Ella, teachers in Japan constantly practice. They do this in particular via an activity called lesson study, which is one of the tenets of Japanese professional development and an idea that has also been used effectively in the United States. In lesson study, a group of teachers plans a lesson together (often on a new topic or employing a new method). Then one of them teaches it in front of the others.

Next comes a feedback session, and then re-planning, and, finally, re-teaching. So not only does lesson study cause teachers to practice together, but it also fosters a culture of feedback and *shared* practice that develops their skills and expertise in the classroom, builds a culture that honors learning and improvement, and instills camaraderie and shared purpose resulting in a sense of shared responsibility.

Another benefit of lesson study is that it allows teachers to practice the two core aspects of their work: lesson delivery—actually getting up and explaining the concepts in a clear and engaging way—and lesson planning—scripting the lesson beforehand to anticipate challenges and design the optimal flow of ideas and activities. As one teacher in an American school that has adopted and adapted lesson study put it, "There is no way to be a good teacher without planning a purposeful approach to every lesson."[7] Lesson study is outstandingly useful because it requires teachers to practice both.

Village Academy Charter School in New York City began implementing lesson study several years ago using a template modeled on the Japanese version—teachers attended a "cycle" of meetings where they defined a topic they were interested in, planned a lesson exploring the topic together, asked one teacher to teach the lesson, spent several hours critiquing the lesson, revised the lesson, and then observed the "final" teaching of the lesson by the same teacher. However, Village Academy also made some adaptations, some of which might seem surprising at first. "We decided to make it voluntary," the school's leader, Deborah Kenny, said. "Those who chose to do it were completely invested, and that's what we wanted. People went above and beyond, and truly gave themselves to the project, and because the people who participated improved so much, the next time around more people wanted to join." The contrast between this "opt-in" approach and requiring professional development sessions is worth considering.

One important result is teachers deciding that they *want* training and that they want it for their own purposes as professionals. Another is that participation becomes an enrichment activity rather than a punishment—someone gives it to you, like a gift, rather than requiring it of you. Finally, it makes it more likely that the culture and camaraderie during the sessions is rigorous and positive through and through.

The assumption that it's better to start with people who want training, ensure that the offering is of extremely high quality, and then let others join in response to the success appears to take a long-term view of improvement, but it also seems especially adaptable to schools and school systems seeking to overcome a precedent of low-value offerings: offering something of quality and letting people ask for more of it changes the cultural dynamic of professional development, which in some cases may be the first step.

Another interesting aspect of the training was the executive's role—almost none. This was a deliberate decision on leadership's part. Kenny explains, "The one essential to good professional development is trusting teachers and giving them room to make mistakes." She wanted to make it clear that lesson study was theirs. But the school also took the results seriously, archiving the model lessons and building them into the curriculum. "In America, a small handful of teachers create textbooks," Kenny said, "but we want our teachers to be scholars and designers and researchers as well. The curriculum will be better if continually refined by teachers as opposed to if they merely carry out what someone else has designed. In so doing, we elevate the profession."

The results were by all accounts transformative. In her book *Born to Rise*, Kenny describes the transformation of a math teacher, Peter. "I didn't see the point of spending a full year working on just one math lesson with four other teachers," Peter recalled. "I was sitting there thinking, 'I already know how to teach this.'" In the end, he found that the training "pushed me to see things I hadn't seen before about how to improve my teaching. Lesson study completely transformed the way I teach."

THEMES FROM THE CASE STUDIES

Several themes connect the two case studies we've examined. First, both were deeply practice-oriented, focusing on rehearsing actions common to the daily life of a teacher. Teachers didn't just talk about what they would do or reflect on what they had done, they *did*—demonstrating in front of their peers, receiving feedback, and then using the feedback to make improvements in additional rounds of practice. The presence of iterative rounds of practice and feedback not only resulted in rapid improvement but also helped build a culture that normalized the giving and using of feedback among peers. The ancillary effects of this in an organization like a school are not hard to imagine.

Second, while both focused on the development of an experienced teacher, they also involved schoolwide sessions that normalized practice, with principals focusing on making it positive and collegial. It was acceptable, even positive, to make mistakes during the practice rounds. Further, new teachers and experienced teachers participated together, practiced together, and improved together, which sends the clear message that practice is something professionals do throughout their careers.

Because the training in both cases focused on practical, daily challenges that were important and germane to teachers—to a large degree, they had helped to identify the things they practiced—it caused teachers to improve in a way that was visible and important to them. Both principals made an effort to show that the practice belongs to the teachers. While they held teachers accountable to varying degrees for what they did with the training, in both cases there were segments of training that were not explicitly supervised, which signaled trust. These aspects made buy-in as well as increased motivation and engagement more likely outcomes.

In both cases, the training was not a "one-off" workshop but a training cycle that involved sustained study of an area of teaching. For this reason, it was more likely to have a tangible result and send the implicit message that the work of solving classroom challenges is intellectually rigorous and worthy of study.

Finally in both cases the training was "by teachers" more than "at teachers," a dynamic that portrays frontline educators as the source of solutions rather than the cause of problems.

BEHIND THE SCENES

It would be easy to imagine a school leaping into professional development earnestly predicated on the above case studies, only to fail spectacularly. If that were to happen, it might be because administrators failed to see the behind-the-scenes work in two key areas that were not immediately visible but that made effective training possible:

Building culture. Both schools constantly stress the importance of a culture among the teaching staff that emphasizes shared endeavor and mutual responsibility (and accountability). But as schools that ask teachers to practice regularly, they also do their best to make it safe to make mistakes by exposing their own mistakes, asking for feedback, and insisting that it be critical, even participating in practice rounds themselves.

As Deborah Kenny points out, schools have to be learning institutions for everybody. "How effective professional development is in a school is a direct result of how effective a leader is in motivating people to learn." Paul Powell, Molly's principal at Troy Prep, often models an activity before his teachers practice it. But when he does so he usually starts by acknowledging that he will need help and feedback to make his modeling better. The sequence usually ends with him getting both positive and constructive feedback from teachers. This signals his willingness to expose his own errors and socializes teachers to do the same.

Hiring for learning. Both schools carefully hired not just for skills but also for the desire to learn. "We want people who want to be good at the work," Paul Powell said. "If they bring that to the table, we think it's our job to make sure they get there." So Powell asks all candidates to teach a sample lesson. But he also gives them feedback to see how they react to it (Do they write it down? Do they ask for more?) and then he often asks them to teach again to see how they use the guidance and how quickly they learn. In some cases he even asks candidates to practice during interview sessions, as he did with a young teacher who seemed promising but who failed to correct an off-task student during her sample.

Powell wanted to make sure the teacher would be able to handle such a student if he trained her in what to do, so he briefed her and asked one of the school's teachers to role-play the student. The teacher got the job and has so far been a success. In short, a good hiring process assesses how fast people will learn from practice by asking them to practice—to try a new skill, to apply feedback and revise, and to see whether they enjoy this process of learning. "If a person is motivated by it, if they like feedback and enjoy getting better and honing their skills, we know they're going to be a match for our culture," Powell said.[8]

RECOMMENDATIONS

- Since professional development works best when it takes school culture into consideration and is embedded in a school's culture, it is ideal for decentralization. Providing flexible funds to building-level leaders would empower them to manage the process more organically.
- Since the data that drive professional development respond to "network effects"—that is, the more people who use them, the more insight there is embedded in the data—developing a data-sharing pool among district and choice schools both within and outside of Milwaukee presents an easy way to learn more, faster.
- The district might also develop additional assessments in areas that are suboptimally assessed (e.g., science and history) so it has information on a wider array of teachers. Similarly, developing shared diagnostic assessments, given periodically across all schools at several points during the school year, would enrich the type and extent of data driving results.
- The district could also decentralize planning by identifying teams of high-performing teachers to help develop materials (e.g., videos, model lesson plans) that could be used across the district to drive training.
- The district could consider contracting outside data analysts to help make sense of the best tools to analyze its data (e.g., regression analysis).
- The district could develop a campaign to shine a light on its best work—both those teachers who perform best— thereby giving them the nonfinancial compensation of praise, honor, and respect—and those schools whose professional development achieves results and buy-in. Positive reinforcement drives behavior as well as or better than negative reinforcement.

- The district could convene a team of leaders (school and central-adminis-
tration based) to consider ways to give teachers more time to practice and
train during the school day.
- The district could give schools video cameras to facilitate taping and
studying top-performing teachers in an informal and day-to-day capacity.

CONCLUSION: IMMENSE PROMISE

The promise of better teacher training is both immense and largely untapped.
In a 2002 study, for example, economist Dan Goldhaber found that "only
about 3 percent of the contribution teachers made to student learning was
associated with teacher experience, degree attained and other readily observ-
able characteristics. The other 97 percent of their contribution was associated
with quality or behaviors that could not be isolated and identified."

In other words 97 percent of what makes teachers effective is related not
to their background and qualifications but to what they do when they are in
the classroom, to their everyday behaviors such as which question to ask or
how to correct a disruptive student. Improving their ability to maximize their
skills and talent in each of those settings is, in the end, the first obligation of
any school or school system.

NOTES

1. "District-by-District Information from the Annual 2012 School Staff Report," http://
dpi.wi.gov/eis/pdf/dpinr2012_58_statewide_data.pdf (accessed May 17, 2013).

2. See "Other Accounts" and "Categorical Programs," FY 2013 Superintendent's Proposed
Budget, www2.milwaukee.k12.wi.us/portal/FY13/Other_Accounts_N.pdf (accessed May 17,
2013), www2.milwaukee.k12.wi.us/portal/FY13/Categorical_Line_Item.pdf (accessed May
17, 2013), and Wisconsin Department of Public Instruction.

3. TNTP's report, *The Irreplaceables*, details the negligence of schools in strategically
retaining their best teachers. "We estimate that in one year alone, at least 10,000 irreplaceables
in the nation's 50 largest school districts left their districts, or left teaching entirely," the study's
authors write. To stem this tide, the three top strategies for better strategic retaining of top-
performing teachers focus on the importance of high-quality professional development and
feedback. Most of these could be accomplished at very little cost by a well-designed professional development program like the one I describe in this chapter. *The Irreplaceables: Understanding the Real Retention Crisis in America's Urban Schools* (Brooklyn: TNTP, 2012).

4. Consider, for example, the study by Springer et al. (2010) in which math teachers were
offered $15,000 bonuses if they were able to improve their students' level of achievement on a
state math test. The incentives resulted in no significant gains. Several critics suggested that
incentives were a flawed idea. In response, Fryer (2011) tried a different approach—offering
group rather than individual incentives—and found a lack of student achievement gains resulted. Drawing on his other incentives research, Fryer notes in his discussion that "teacher
incentives that have been tested in American schools uniformly incentivize student learning
outputs." Such studies assume teachers inherently know effective ways to increase student
achievement, which, Fryer notes dryly, "is not necessarily the case." Fryer continues: "One
explanation is that teachers are responding to the incentives, but in counterproductive ways. If a
teacher invests excess time into practices or interventions that are less efficient in producing

student achievement than their normal practices, we would expect especially motivated and misinformed teachers to overinvest time in ineffective practices at the expense of student learning." Motivating teachers doesn't work when they don't know *how* to be better. M. G. Springer, L. Hamilton, D. F. McCaffrey, D. Ballou, V. N. Le, M. Pepper et al., *Teacher Pay for Performance: Experimental Evidence from the Project on Incentives in Teaching* (Nashville, TN: National Center on Performance Incentives, Vanderbilt University, 2010); Roland G. Fryer Jr., *Teacher Incentives and Student Achievement: Evidence from New York City Public Schools* (Cambridge: Harvard University, Department of Economics, 2011).

5. Karen Hawley Miles, Allan Odden, Mark Fermanich, Sarah Archibald, and Alix Gallagher, "An Analysis of Professional Development Spending in Four Districts Using a New Cost Framework," *Consortium for Policy Research in Education*, Working Paper Series (Madison, WI: University of Wisconsin-Madison, 2002), http://cpre.wceruw.org/papers/4DistrictPD_SF.pdf (accessed May 17, 2013).

6. Specifically, 50 percent of teachers in high-poverty schools leave within the first five years, and in some urban districts, this timeframe can be as short as three years. M. Haberman, *Star Teachers of Children in Poverty* (Indianapolis: Kappa Delta Pi, 1995).

7. Deborah Kenny, *Born to Rise: A Story of Children and Teachers Reaching Their Highest Potential* (New York: Harper Collins Publishers, 2012).

8. See Nair, this volume, for a longer discussion on recruitment, hiring, and human-capital management.

Chapter Five

Building a Better Pipeline

Thinking Smarter about Talent Management

Ranjit Nair

Teacher effectiveness is the single most important factor in maximizing student academic achievement.[1] But *teacher effectiveness* is still an ill-defined concept. Many school districts include this same basic goal in their strategic plan: "Ensure every classroom has a high-quality, effective educator, supported by high-quality, effective administrators and support staff." However, without sufficient time, knowledge, and investment in fostering, harnessing, and shaping a high-performance culture, the results of strategic plans, including a human-capital management plan, often fall short of expectations and aspirations.

This chapter presents a series of strategies to strengthen human-capital management in an effort to help districts pursue the goals of greater academic achievement, increased college readiness, and lower school drop-out rates. Better recruitment techniques, increased rigor in performance management, and strategically aligned compensation management must be integrated within a district to create, nourish, and sustain a high-performance culture in schools. A human-capital management strategy is directly linked to unleashing a high-performance organizational culture—both within the district and within the schools themselves.

The chapter proposes a redesigned human-capital strategy to be implemented in perennially underperforming urban school districts like Milwaukee. Each of the strategy's elements—many of which are derived from traditional business-sector practices—will be described, and the application of business strategies to the school environment will be explored and discussed. The chapter concludes with a series of action items required at the state and local level in order for the proposed human-capital management plan to be effectively adopted and executed in an urban school context.

CRITICAL SUCCESS FACTORS TO BUILDING A WINNING CULTURE

A 2007 groundbreaking study conducted by McKinsey comparing twenty-five of the world's school systems, including ten of the top performers, identified three elements critical for success:

- getting the right people to become teachers;
- developing them into effective instructors; and
- ensuring that the system is able to deliver the best possible instruction for every child. [2]

In what follows, I describe the core principles of a successful, integrated human-capital strategy designed to facilitate a school system's engagement in these necessary activities. An integrated human-capital strategy is one in which all people and all human-resources functions—from recruitment, selection, and career and professional development to succession planning and compensation—are linked and seamlessly intertwined.

Such a strategy must also encompass the entire employee life cycle within the system (i.e., from hire to retire). The ultimate goal of such a strategy is to foster a high-performance culture in which teachers, principals, administrators, and other employees understand and pursue the shared goals of the community and the institutions they serve in the context of individual accountability.

A human-capital strategy cannot be the single answer, nor is it a silver bullet for the numerous challenges plaguing education today. It can, however, promote a high-performance organizational culture that can positively influence student learning, workplace satisfaction, and the overall impact of education. The creation and sustenance of a high-performance culture through a human-capital perspective entails the following steps and requires that the associated questions be posed and answered:

- Identifying specific individual competencies, qualifications, and characteristics sought in high-performing employees. *Question: Which skills and behaviors are we looking for?*
- Creating a sourcing and hiring strategy to attract candidates with these qualities. *Question: How are we going to attract those people and where do we find them?*

- Creating a talent-management process that retains high performers and develops employees to fill critical positions, in particular in high-need schools. *Question: How do we ensure that high-performing employees continue to perform at these levels?*
- Establishing a performance-management system in which objectives are clearly agreed upon, understood, and measured. *Question: What methodology do we use to track individual progress?*
- Establishing a compensation philosophy that promotes high performance. *Question: How do we differentiate individual performance and reward accordingly?*
- Establishing a performance dashboard with clear, relevant, and easily understood metrics. *Question: Which data and human-capital metrics should be tracked?*

RECRUITMENT STRATEGY

The nation faces a daunting teacher shortage, especially in specific high-demand areas such as math, science, special education, and bilingual education. The U.S. Department of Education estimates that school districts will need to hire more than 2 million new teachers over the next ten years.[3] While individual schools can attempt to attract the right caliber of teacher candidates, it is a system-level or broader (state and/or federal) strategy that can raise the status of teaching as a high-paying, noble, and personally rewarding profession and, subsequently, enhance the quality of individuals entering this profession. Raising the overall status of the profession within the community should be the primary goal for the school system at a district or state level in order for any recruiting strategy to work.

The United States was the first country to offer every young person the opportunity to obtain a free public secondary education at the end of the nineteenth and beginning of the twentieth century, and, in turn, the country realized tremendous economic rewards and outcomes. Yet, the sad truth is that today, the United States has lost this edge. Countries such as South Korea, Singapore, Finland, Norway, Japan, and Canada have leapfrogged over the United States in terms of improvements in education outcomes.

One reason for this is how these leading countries recruit talent. Teacher and principal candidates are treated with reverence, and, in most cases, these potential recruits see teaching opportunities as phenomenal and foundational to the needs of their countries. In fact, teachers are regarded as nation-builders because they are seen as the sages who develop youth to lead and drive the enhancement of economic outcomes for their respective countries.

In the recruiting process, these candidates have to undergo very challenging hurdles such as passing a competency-based interview or test. In Finland, for example, it is a tremendous honor to be a teacher, and teachers are afforded a status comparable to what doctors, lawyers, and other highly regarded professionals enjoy in the United States; only one out of every ten applicants makes it into the Finnish training pool for teachers.[4]

In Singapore as well, there is a competitive and highly selective recruiting strategy that endeavors to build its own sense of professional conduct and meet high standards for skills development. Singapore carefully sources and selects its candidates from the top one-third of the secondary school graduating class. While still in school, they receive a monthly stipend that is competitive with the monthly salary for fresh graduates in other fields. In exchange, they must commit to teaching for at least three years. This investment is seen as a need to truly differentiate which candidates are most suited for the honorable and nationalistic task of developing the leaders of the future.

Research has shown that very important determinants of attracting high-performing teachers and maintaining that performance are the ways teachers feel about their professional identity and the local teaching culture shaping their views and expectations regarding work. Hence, careful attention should be paid to the individual identification models for existing teachers and the organizational culture fostering them. In order to be able to attract the right quality of teachers, administrators, and leadership for the schools in the district, the identification of "what good looks like" is essential. This should be defined at the district level and cascaded to all the individual schools as a part of their hiring, performance-management, and talent-management processes.

In the author's experience as a twenty-year veteran of human-resource management in the business sector, figure 5.1 would provide a good benchmark for determining "what good looks like" when seeking to identify the highest-caliber candidates to fill the recruitment pipeline. Most organizations today identify what their ideal employee should look like based on his/her knowledge, skills, and attitudes.

While knowledge and skills can be deciphered through individuals' qualifications and experience, competencies, in many ways, are behavioral indicators and give a clear idea, if not a complete picture, of individuals' attitudes. Most public schools do not use such rigor in the hiring process; job descriptions are typically outdated or are based on old templates that are no longer useful, and they lack a holistic view for what is needed to hire the best and the brightest.

SOURCING STRATEGY

Public schools traditionally hire their teachers from other schools or school systems, or they hire recently minted graduates from university programs. Teacher-training institutions may well continue to be the primary source of

Role	Qualifications	Competencies
Teachers	• Teachers who teach seventh through 12th grade math, science, history or English must hold a master's degree in the subject. • Classroom or homeroom teachers or those teaching in elementary school must hold a master's degrees in general education.	• Initiative and commitment • Empathy • Influence and negotiation • Achievement orientation and motivation to learn. • Detail-oriented • Cultural awareness • Effective communication and interpersonal ability • Emotional intelligence • Problem-solving and decision-making • Coaching and mentoring
Leadership team and administrators	• A business degree or certification • Experience managing team of knowledge workers • Project management skills	In addition to the above: • Strategic thinking • Leadership • Innovation

Figure 5.1.   Suggested Rubric for Recruiting in Public Schools

hires, as they are now. However, unless state authorities implement or mandate a system that tests, evaluates, and selects teachers even before they start their teacher training, the status of the teaching profession and the quality of teachers will not improve. This is particularly important in Wisconsin, where University of Wisconsin System schools of education generally have lower admission requirements than other schools in the system.

A strenuous screening and training process ensures that the teachers with the right competencies and motivation enter education schools and the classroom. Basic skill levels are met and a sense of pride and achievement directly correlate with being selected for teacher training. Exemplars, both Singapore and Finland, have put systems in place wherein selection to a teacher-training course or degree program is exclusive and limited to the top 30 and 20 percent, respectively, of academic achievers.

Conversely, the minimum qualifying Praxis II score in Wisconsin, for example, is well below the national median score and is set somewhat below the level of some other states even though the average score of candidates is higher than the national average.[5] Moreover, retaining a low minimum score requirement undermines the pride in getting accepted to such programs.

Public relations and community awareness as well as internal and external marketing communications need to be pitched at high levels in order to appeal to the different types of potential talent that need to be attracted to schools. These targets could be fresh graduates, experienced hires, volunteers, and retirees. The training and development agencies for public schools in the United Kingdom, for example, have tracked marketing and public relations campaigns and rolled out targeted branding that engages different source groups, for example, volunteers, students, senior executives, young graduates, etcetera.

In the United States, these types of marketing and advertising campaigns should be conducted at the state or federal level initially. Additionally, in many ways, this approach mirrors the strategy used by many blue-chip business organizations that not only hire experienced professionals but also indulge in campus recruitment and compete vigorously to attract the highest talent to their organizations.

It is an imperative to hire people who believe in the school system and teaching philosophy and who have the same vision and want to teach. Teachers should be taught and expected to have an education philosophy in place that also espouses their personal stake and involvement in building a high-performing culture in the institutions they serve. According to the results of a 2010 McKinsey study that was developed for the United States to learn about what high-performing countries are doing in public education, Finland, which has virtually no low-performing schools,[6] also has a vigorous methodology before individuals can even enter the teacher-training program. The best candidates go through a series of interviews to judge their "fit" for teaching based on factors such as motivation and emotional intelligence.

Targeting top executives of local and national businesses that may be nearing retirement and appealing to their philanthropic calling would be a source for acquiring talent. Volunteer teaching has been used successfully in many school districts, including Milwaukee, Houston, and Denver; however, there is huge untapped potential here that needs to be explored. The best way to accelerate and instill a culture of performance is to infiltrate the schools with like-minded individuals with experience doing this and the passion to contribute to their communities.

In other words, school systems should hire personnel from the business sector with deep experience in world-class talent-acquisition strategies. These individuals can contribute to the school system, sharing their well-honed corporate management skills with educators and administrators. Their involvement in the school activities may also have a larger social impact, encouraging greater community participation in the activities of local schools.

An employee referral program is a tool used in many high-performing Fortune 500 companies and is especially useful in attracting individuals who will align with a high-performing culture. The assumption is that people will refer their friends to join the company if they themselves feel engaged and satisfied working at that company. If teachers refer their friends to the school, more often than not they would be of a caliber the referrer will be confident to be associated with.

Corporations generally have a modest reward and recognition attached with a successful hire from an internal employee. This can easily be translated to schools, as well, and may be particularly helpful in finding people to fill specialized subject areas. An employee referral program reduces recruitment costs, increases retention, and provides a higher performance rate for new employees. But such a simple tool is rarely used in U.S. public school systems.

SCREENING TECHNIQUE

Sifting through numerous resumes can be a tedious process even with state-of-the art recruiting systems. This process should include not only identifying academic qualifications and skills, but also utilizing a competency-based assessment technique whose results should be aligned to identify the best possible candidate for that position. For higher-need schools or districts such as those in low-income areas, hiring principals and teachers may require different skills and experiences as well as the aforementioned competencies to be successful. This variation should be embraced and recognized, and a human-capital tactic targeting these needs should be applied as part of the overarching human-capital strategy. This will help ensure that the person selected fits the role.

Employee "fit" is a concept that should form the centerpiece of a world-class recruiting process within a high-performance organizational culture. One of the most common barriers is the concept of one-size-fits-all, which tends to discount the finer competencies that are essential to meet the specific requirements of the school. Many school districts look for typical baseline skills and credentials such as a degree, certification, and teaching experience but most do not use a rigorous competency-based model for hiring.

It is imperative that school systems review the competencies and behaviors stipulated for any given role or open position and base their hiring on these and any other specific requirements. Such a competency-based recruitment (CBR) strategy is required in high-performing organizational cultures.

CBR is a process of recruitment based on the ability of candidates (teachers, principals, administrators) to produce anecdotes about their public school and other relevant experience that can be used as evidence that the candidate has a given competency. This competency should be one of an established set of competencies that the district has articulated as part of a wish list. Potential candidates demonstrate competencies on the application form, and once again during the competency-based interview.

The process is intended to be fairer while at the same time also more relevant and purposeful than existing practices in public schools. Currently in Milwaukee, Teach For America, which operates in several private and public schools, as well as several charter schools (including some authorized by the Milwaukee Public Schools), engages in some type of CBR. However, it remains the exception rather than the rule in most Milwaukee schools.

The Houston Independent School District, in contrast, employs a systemic CBR process by clearly laying down the required competencies and then testing them in such a way that the district's recruiter has little discretion to favor one candidate over another. The practice in underperforming school systems allows too much recruiter discretion, and that is both undesirable and detrimental to the pursuit of a high-performing human-capital strategy.

CBR is highly focused on the candidates' story-telling abilities as an indication of competency, and disfavors other indications of a candidate's skills and potential, such as credentials and references. For example, in high-need schools, *resilience* may be an essential human competency—the ability to be resourceful under difficult situations, as in schools located in low-income regions. Ensuring also that the best person for the role is hired "the first time right" ensures that cost of hiring is managed and controlled. The worst that could occur is that the person hired fails in the role or fails to get onboard successfully in a short time. This creates havoc and chaos in the school and also has a deep financial and emotional impact on the school district, the community, and the students.

SELECTING

A combination of selection (hiring) methods helps in identifying the right candidate for the role. These could include:

- assessment centers, including a practical classroom teaching demonstration;
- psychometric testing; and
- structured competency-based interview techniques.

Implementing a robust selection process for hiring the best candidate is an integral part of talent acquisition. Most schools typically identify several potential candidates after they have gone through the screening process. But the challenge lies in selecting the candidate with the best fit for the role.

A minimum requirement standard identified by the school system at the district level in terms of both qualifications and behavioral competencies

Principal competency	Application form	Resume screening	Screening interview	In-person interview
Communicating and influencing — Communicates information effectively to a wide range of diverse stakeholders (students, peers, parents, supervisors, administrators, community leaders), influencing events			x	x
Organization and delivery — Plans time effectively to achieve results in day-to-day schoolwork. Is organized and prioritizes activities appropriately	x		x	
Team working — Works effectively as a member of a team. Takes responsibility for getting things done as part of a team.	x			x
Adaptability — Responds positively to change, supporting others in managing transition and being flexible in approaches to role. Is aware of own strengths and areas for development. Seeks feedback on own work.	x			x

Figure 5.2   Example of a Competency-Based Recruitment Tool

needs to be set as a baseline. Each school should review this list and add to it specific behaviors or skill sets unique to the school and the role it is seeking to fill.

The specific behavioral competencies and skills for the specific role should be identified for the role. Shortlisted candidates should then be matched against these standards and minimum requirements as well as the critical competencies required for the role. They should then be ranked. Pursuant to successful background checks, the offer should be made according to the ranking.

PERFORMANCE MANAGEMENT

Performance management needs to be implemented through both a structured evaluative and a developmental process. Setting individual performance goals at the outset of the school year is imperative to set the tone for the new performance-based culture. The initial step in the performance-management process is to establish five to seven performance targets. This step must be completed no later than the first month of the school year.

Setting the goals should be a collaborative dialogue that occurs between, say, the principal and the teacher who reports to her. Selecting five to seven goals for the school year gives the individual a sense of purpose and focus, while also executing the overarching human-capital strategy. In the business sector, most high-performing organizations try to help employees to work on the most important objectives to achieve overall organizational success. But performance tends to wane if there are too many goals to execute.

The Miami-Dade County Public Schools suggest a looped process consisting of three activities dispersed throughout the year. These activities include the setting of performance targets within the first month of the school year, conducting midyear performance reviews before the winter break, and conducting performance evaluations at the end of the school year. These three steps are fundamental to creating a performance-based culture and add a much-needed rigor to the process.

In addition, at least three formal midterm "check-ins" should take place between the principal and the teacher to give both parties a sense of what has been achieved, what is on target to be achieved, and what will not be achieved. At the same time, the principal can get a very strong sense for differentiating the performance of the teacher against the agreed-upon goals. Additionally, the principal can rank and compare performance between teachers. A performance-management system with clear standards and criteria executed well by evaluators (principals or administrators) against those criteria helps create the necessary *differentiation*—arguably, the most critical component of a pay-for-performance program.

An effective performance-management system needs:

- *A clear statement of goals and expected outcomes defined for the district so that each school and employee understands how he or she contributes to the larger picture.*
- *A set of objectives based on the strategic focus for the school for that academic year, for example, reducing dropout rates in high school by a certain percentage.*

The objectives hence need to be "SMART": Specific, Measurable, Achievable, Relevant, and Time-bound. The SMART principles are widely used to define objectives and set goals in a clear and articulate manner.

The Commonwealth of Virginia's Education Department emphasizes the use of SMART goals for its teachers and encourages them to focus their attention on instructional improvement based on a process of determining what baseline performance is, developing and implementing strategies for improvement, and then assessing the results at the conclusion of the academic year. In the vein of a high-performance culture incorporating *continuous improvement*, the bar is set higher each year going forward. Here is an example of how SMART goals are used there for improving student math skills:

- *School's goal:* Every student will show evidence of one year of growth in mathematics each year in attendance.
- *SMART goal:* During the 2011–2012 school year, all students will improve their math problem-solving skills as measured by a one-year gain in national grade-equivalent growth from the 2010–2011 to the 2011–2012 math problem-solving subtest.
- *School's goal:* Reduce levels of nonproficient students by 10 percent in all grades on standardized-test math concepts and estimation.
- *SMART goal:* During the 2011–2012 school year, nonproficient students (as indicated by the standardized math concepts and estimation subtest) at Sample School will improve their math concepts and estimation skills by 5 percent as measured by an increase in the percentage of students scoring in the "high" and "proficient" levels on the standardized-test math concepts and estimation subtest.

- *Explicit expectations that include images of satisfactory and exemplary performance (e.g., videos of classroom practice, annotated student work, samples of teacher feedback) to help set the performance bar high and encourage improvement*: Hillsborough County reported that online videos of exemplary practice were an important resource for teachers learning about the district's expectations.[7]
- *Performance management directed to the leadership and administrative team as well as teachers*: For example, in Charlotte-Mecklenburg, the superintendent set annual goals that were tied to school-level improvement. The executive team was required to identify five "critical disparities" that were linked to these goals, and each executive team member was evaluated in terms of progress toward achieving them. Such an evaluation system began only with district leadership and over time was to be phased in for the rest of the district- and school-level faculty and staff.[8]
- *A dashboard of key performance indicators for individuals based on their roles, that is, leadership versus the teaching track.* For example, there might be a number of initiatives to encourage students to participate at state-level competitions. Other metrics given at the end of this chapter can also be used to track high performance.

Creating the right measures has no single best-practice formula, and what is important is that all stakeholders agree that the measure is what they want to achieve. It would be helpful to clearly define what constitutes low performance (e.g., a 5 percent increase in student learning rates is good; however, less than 3 percent would be considered poor).

- *Multiple evaluative methods to give a more holistic measure of teacher performance*: This would include feedback from colleagues, heads of departments, parents, and students separate from the key performance indicators set out in the performance goals.
- *Focused support on a school and state level for development of the individuals*: High-performing schools typically will spend more time having performance conversations with teachers in order to ultimately increase performance standards. Some of these essential performance conversations are articulated in figure 5.3.

A good recruitment strategy along with a strong performance-management culture will contribute to more robust talent management and ultimately stronger engagement. All of this will lead to a high-performing human-capital system.

Annual review meeting	Points of Discussion
Performance against the agreed objectives	• What were your key achievements? • What areas need improvement? • Were there any barriers to your performance? • Have you done any special project, i.e., worked above and beyond the defined objectives? • What is your performance rating for the year?
Review of the annual objectives	• What are your specific individual goals; what are the school's goals? • Are any current objectives irrelevant?
Continuous professional development discussion	Consider development needs to: • Expand and update on strengths and subject matter expertise • Address areas requiring improvement • Meet future challenges and/or aspirations • Identify avenues of continuous learning
Review level of engagement and gain feedback	• What gives you the most satisfaction at work? Did this year provide you opportunity for that? • How can we ensure you maintain or improve your satisfaction? • How is your pay determined, and how do you earn an incentive? • What are your final rewards for performance?

Figure 5.3. Performance Management Guidelines

STRATEGIC COMPENSATION MANAGEMENT

Strategic compensation management has been a tactic deployed by many high-performing school districts. (For more on how to evaluate compensation systems to make the best use of resources, see Travers, Green, and Hawley Miles, this volume.) A better or more appropriate way to describe such programs is "pay for performance."

Currently, performance-related pay programs are attracting more and more attention as evidenced by the development of programs such as Denver's ProComp, Houston's ASPIRE, and the U.S. Department of Education's Teacher Incentive Fund. Some of the most prominent performance-related pay programs are found in Texas, where the Governor's Educator Excellence Award Program awards over $300 million in grants through the Texas Educator Excellence Grant and the Governor's Educator Excellence Grant.

These compensation programs are designed to build a strategic system of teacher compensation by adding an "at-risk" element of pay to existing compensation with the goals of making a positive impact on teacher pay reform, improving teacher quality, and increasing student achievement.

The Austin Independent School System began implementing its audacious pay-for-performance program, AISD REACH, in July 2007. The program targeted three key areas for the school system: student growth, professional growth, and recruitment and retention of teachers and principals at highest-need schools. It combined three components: an outcome-based, pay-for-performance component based on student achievement measures with two input-based components—one for professional development and another for teaching in hard-to-staff schools. The district's goals for this program were to place a quality teacher in every classroom, particularly in Austin's highest-need schools, to improve student learning at all schools for all students, to achieve professional growth for teachers, and to increase retention of teachers and principals. [9]

These incentive awards were in addition to what the teachers, principals, and other staff earned in base salary and ranged from $1,500 to $15,000. Many school systems around the country have implemented or are implementing such programs hoping to emulate the success seen in such programs from the business sector. It is widely believed that current teacher-compensation practices do not adequately match the diverse and rapidly changing needs of today's public education system. In particular, the widely used single salary schedule may no longer be the most suitable way to compensate teachers.

The results of this program are still being assessed, but early indications are that the program has had lukewarm success, with challenges stemming from lack of understanding of the program by its participants, lack of communication of how it works and why it is being implemented, and the lack of rigor in setting individual goals in the performance-management process.

The results of a comprehensive evaluation of the program conducted by researchers at Vanderbilt University's Peabody College of Education[10] showed that AISD REACH respondent teachers themselves expressed only moderate support for pay-for-performance in general. Thus, while the program was led by good intentions, the execution of the plan was inadequate, and the district missed an opportunity to leverage strategic compensation as a driver of performance.

For strategic compensation initiatives to succeed, the goals of the program must be clearly articulated and each component explained in terms of how it relates to the overarching human-capital strategy. Additionally, the key leaders in the system—the superintendent, the senior human-resources manager, the principals, and the senior teachers—must all engage in dialogue around pay-for-performance.

Pay needs to be demystified, especially if strategic compensation is being piloted. At every opportunity, these key stakeholders must provide feedback to program participants about what the incentive opportunities are, why they are set at the levels they are, what the key performance indicators are, and, at the end, what reward was given and why that amount.

The key to strategic pay for performance plans lies in the ability of the performance-rater to differentiate performance and also differentiate pay rewards accordingly. If the highest performer receives similar incentives to a weaker performer, the strategy will have failed. The very best performers should be surprised and elated by the reward, thereby producing a "wow" experience for him or her. Even more important, they should know why they received the reward. A "wow" experience occurs in pay-for-performance programs within high-performing organizational cultures where the recipient of an incentive award is impressed by the size of the award and knows that her performance was truly recognized as exemplary and outstanding relative to her peers.

It is imperative that the very best performers are paid this kind of attention through differentiated rewards. In other words, the high performer has exceeded in all aspects of the five to seven objectives set forth earlier in the year and has now been recognized through rewards for that level of performance. Finally, in order to sustain a high-performance culture, these very best performers who have earned high-incentive rewards should be integrated into other human-capital initiatives such as a career and professional development and succession planning. The future of the organization rests in the continued development of this best and brightest talent.

ACTION POINTS: A WAY FORWARD

Once put in place, the above strategies need to be continuously monitored, tracked, and improved upon. Gauging effectiveness of these programs can be accomplished by instilling a *measurement focus* as part of the governance processes. A dashboard indicating the success of the measures is essential for this. As an example, school principals can present this type of dashboard to showcase the performance of their school against the human-capital strategy, and superintendents could share this type of dashboard analytics with their boards. Below are a series of recommendations that can be incorporated into such a dashboard.

Inculcation of a high-performance culture is a journey. Organizational culture can be created and managed, albeit with a focused vision and leadership. Schools, like their business counterparts, have an external image that needs to be managed and cultivated, while also having a functional element that is measured based on performance, quality, safety, market share, profitability, etcetera. For schools and the school system, this functional element undoubtedly has to be performance-oriented as well. This functional element is emphasized through a series of internal actions, processes, tools, programs, rituals, and artifacts that may be less visible to outsiders but are clear, present, and visible as part of a culture within the schools themselves.

The entire education community must be effectively engaged if a human-capital initiative is to be successful. Messages around human-capital initiatives and processes should be clear, vivid, and aligned to the district's and the school's overarching strategic plan. Hence as a start, a strategy defining where the school system wants to see itself in one year or five years should be articulated.

Focus areas for the year must be identified, agreed upon, and cascaded to the various schools within the district. Every employee in the school system must be made aware of this strategy and, most importantly, everyone should know how his/her work impacts this strategy. For example, in 2010 Utah's Park City School District released its strategic plan laying out the vision, mission, and values guiding its strategic focus areas and objectives. An example of a strategic objective linked to instruction was, "Attract, develop, retain and support caring, motivated, innovative, engaging and professional faculty and staff." The various performance measures (as identified in figure 5.4, "Key Metrics") linked to the objective were then identified.

This integrated and bold talent-acquisition strategy should include the steps needed to enable the district to identify, recruit, and appoint teachers and administrators who have the specific qualifications and competencies identified as critical by the district and who believe in the district philosophy. Recruitment should not just be about filling roles with qualified professionals but rather finding the right "fit" or match in the type of hire that is required

Percentage of employees rated below standard, standard and above standard performance	% of employees with a specific rating/total number of employees rated	This is essential to manage expectations for the next academic year and differentiate teacher performance wisely.
High-performer turnover	% of high-performer leavers/average high-performer population	Average high-performer population = number of high performers in the beginning of the time period + the number of high performers at the end of the period/2
Percentage of dropouts relative to number of students within measurement period	% of total number of dropouts in an academic year/total number of students in the academic year	Dropouts = students who start at the beginning of the academic year but do not continue
Percentage of graduates satisfied with the usefulness of their education in achieving their goals after graduation	% of graduates who are satisfied/total number of graduates who responded to the survey	Graduates = students who graduated at least one year prior. Survey to be sent to these alumni.
Percentage of academic staff with a master's	% of academic staff with master's degrees/total number of academic staff	An alternate measure: % of academic staff with master's degrees/total number of roles that have been defined to need master's degrees as a prerequisite.
Ratio of administrative staff to students	% of students enrolled/total number of administrative staff and services	This is a productivity measure, and target would be to improve this gradually.
Increase in student scores in two consecutive examination sessions (learning rate)	Difference in average scores from one examination to another	Target learning rates need to be defined and be a part of individual teachers' and principals' key performance indicators.
Engagement score	This would be based on engagement surveys on the lines of the Gallup Engagement Survey	The target would be to increase the score every survey year.

Figure 5.4. Key Metrics

for a particular role. Leadership theorist and author Simon Sinek has posited, "If you hire people just because they can do a job, they'll work for your money. But if you hire people who believe what you believe, they'll work for you with blood and sweat and tears."[11]

The defined strategy would then need local school principals and administrators to ensure that the performance objectives for the year for individual teachers are aligned with the overall strategy. For this to be effective and make a difference, school systems like Milwaukee need to include other stakeholders such as unions, state legislative units, university systems, and corporate stakeholders within the community to help build this integrated high-performance culture.

The above narration illustrates how a school system's organizational culture can be developed through an integrated human-capital strategy that seamlessly implements a purposeful plan of action incorporating recruiting practices, performance-managing, and rewarding that are communicated well and that engage employees across the system and schools to ultimately create and sustain a high-performance culture.

NOTES

1. K. Ballard and A. Bates, "Making a Connection between Student Achievement, Teacher Accountability and Quality Classroom Instruction," *The Qualitative Report* 13, no. 4 (December 2008): 560–580.

2. M. Barber and M. Mourshed, *How the World's Best-Performing School Systems Come Out on Top* (New York: McKinsey & Company, 2007).

3. Mark C. Schug and M. Scott Niederjohn, *Preparing Effective Teachers for the Milwaukee Public Schools* (Thiensville: Wisconsin Policy Research Institute, 2008).

4. Barber and Mourshed, *How the World's Best-Performing School Systems,* 16.

5. Schug and Niederjohn, *Preparing Effective Teachers.*

6. Betsy Brown Ruzzi, *Finland Education Report* (Washington, DC: National Center on Education and the Economy, 2005).

7. W. Ross and A. Jacobs, *Designing and Implementing Teacher Performance Management Systems* (Washington, DC: Aspen Institute, 2011).

8. Ross and Jacobs, *Designing and Implementing.*

9. Ross and Jacobs, *Designing and Implementing.*

10. S. Burns, C. Gardner, and J. Meeuwsen, "An Evaluation of Teacher and Principal Experiences during the Pilot Phase of AISD REACH, A Strategic Compensation Initiative," National Center on Performance Incentives, Policy Evaluation Report, August 2009.

11. Simon Sinek, *Start with Why* (New York: Penguin Group, 2009).

Chapter Six

Spare Some Change

Smarter District Resource Use for
Transformational Schools

Jonathan Travers, Genevieve Green,
and Karen Hawley Miles

Urban districts across the country are at a crossroads. They face still another year of cuts in federal, state, and local revenue along with new teacher-evaluation systems and the implementation of Common Core standards. Meanwhile, expectations for student performance are higher. Many districts—like Milwaukee Public Schools—are experiencing declining enrollment and competition from charters and other schools. In response to lower levels of funding, districts typically cut central office services, freeze wages, and require staff to take furlough days. Doing less with less, however, is unlikely to bring about the transformation necessary to dramatically improve student outcomes.

Education Resource Strategies (ERS) works with large urban school districts to help identify the resource reallocations necessary to create high-performing schools at scale. We've seen the bright spots firsthand—in school districts like Baltimore City, Charlotte, and Denver—where district leaders are breaking away from traditional cost structures and working to align their use of talent, time, and technology with a transformed vision for the future. Through this work, we've developed a framework that describes Seven Strategies for District Transformation.[1] These strategies can free districts from unproductive resource use and enable investment in higher-performing designs for schools and systems.

This chapter explores the school funding system—how the district allocates resources to schools—as one of the most immediately impactful strategies for districts like Milwaukee Public Schools. We identify the characteristics of an effective funding system and the critical design features that help ensure that MPS's funding strategy—alongside other transformational strategies—supports high performance across all schools. We also offer insight into the most important policy and funding barriers that state and other non-district stakeholders will need to address for districts like MPS to successfully transform.

SCHOOL FUNDING SYSTEMS

Urban school districts should employ school funding systems—mechanisms, policies, and processes that allocate dollars and staffing resources to schools—that are guided by three core principles: equity, flexibility, and transparency.[2] Most school districts allocate specific staff positions to schools based on the number of students they have. But, in times when school organizations are changing rapidly with the introduction of new ways of grouping students or technology and where school designs vary widely across schools, systems that allocate staff become tricky to administer and compare. Weighted Student Funding (WSF), the system Milwaukee uses, can help enable equity, flexibility, and transparency. But whether WSF accomplishes these goals depends on how it's implemented.

Equitable school funding systems ensure that students who have greater needs, such as those who are English Language Learners or those who require special education services, get more resources to match the cost of extra support (known as "vertical equity") and that students with similar needs receive similar levels of resources regardless of what school they attend (known as "horizontal equity").

Funding systems that allocate staff positions based on one-size-fits-all staffing ratios (1 counselor per 550 students) applied across diverse school portfolios typically do not account for differentiated levels of student need. In addition, models that allocate the same position sets (i.e., a principal, assistant principal, instructional coach, school social worker, and secretary) across all schools typically end up spending more—sometimes significantly more—per pupil in their smallest schools. Similarly, districts that hold large portions of school resources centrally and allocate them based on the preferences and objectives of individual departments (i.e., the Department of Teaching and Learning budgeting and deploying the district's instructional coaches) can also have difficulty ensuring that schools' *total* allocations are commensurate to need.

As a district using WSF, MPS allocates dollars on a per-pupil basis rather than positions, and utilizes higher weights for students with higher levels of need. Choices about which students get weighted how much should reflect the district's beliefs about which student characteristics require additional resources for students to meet desired outcomes.

While these typically include ELL, special education, and free/reduced lunch status, they can also include school-level weightings if the district believes the outcomes desired at different school grade levels require different resource investment levels. Publicly available MPS FY13 budget documents indicate that, for example, MPS weights high school students at 1.17, which equates to an additional $666 per pupil to reflect MPS's intention of pushing additional resources to high school students.[3] While different types of funding systems can lead to equitable distribution of resources, WSF typically offers districts a clear pathway to achieving greater funding equity across many different types of schools.

Equal dollars do not necessarily translate to equal resources. The unequal distribution of effective teachers across the district and the historical neglect of infrastructure in certain schools cause inequities to persist in spite of fair funding weights. Furthermore, getting the financial resource levels "right" across schools and students does limited good unless those schools have the ability to use them based on their unique needs and instructional models. Therefore, strategic funding systems also seek to be flexible—to give school leaders the authority to match allocated funding to specific school needs. This means ensuring that school leaders have the ability to reallocate spending when necessary, make scheduling changes, swap staff positions, and hire teachers and other staff who best fit the school.

Tailoring to specific needs is particularly important when a district's schools vary widely in size and student characteristics, and when a district seeks to foster innovative ways of organizing resources. Traditional, ratio-based funding systems can try to achieve this by offering principals the ability to "swap" positions or to convert them to dollars to fund non-personnel resources.

WSF systems—by giving schools dollars rather than positions—appear to offer greater flexibility to schools to design staffing configurations and budgets that match their specific needs. However, as we've seen in our work across the country, policies that mandate specific resource models (e.g., Florida's K–3 class-size max of eighteen) can severely limit the true flexibility schools ultimately experience. (For more on innovation and barriers to achieving it, see Horn and Evans, this volume.)

Finally, strategic funding systems are transparent. Stakeholders know how much each school receives and understand the basis for the allocation. This means ensuring that funding can be traced to the level of individual schools and that clearly documented procedures on central and school-level budgeting exist. ERS has found that districts with less than 70 percent of total budgets reported at the school level often fail to provide the transparency needed to determine whether resources are used effectively. This can foster mistrust among stakeholders, make it hard to assess true equity and flexibility, and hinder leadership's ability to make informed resource allocation choices across the system.

Although WSF can be a good approach for increasing equity, flexibility, and transparency in a school district, four critical design factors influence its success. MPS, like other urban districts that employ this funding strategy, should consider the following five questions:

- *How differentiated are the weights assigned to specific student populations, and do different weights reflect students' relative needs?* Within the weight assigned to students with special needs, students who require more intensive services should receive a larger allocation than those who do not. Additional student populations should also receive differentiated weights, particularly incoming students in general education at the secondary levels who are at least two grade levels behind.

  Sufficiently differentiating student weights will increase the likelihood that a district's weighted student-funding formula reinforces equitable resource use. In Baltimore City, district leaders implemented a WSF system that deliberately over-weighted its special education inclusion model relative to self-contained as a means of incentivizing schools to shift to less restrictive environments.[4]

- *What percentage of the district's total budget runs through the funding formula?* Weights that impact per-pupil allocation only influence dollars that are run through the relevant formula. It's reasonable to expect some funding to remain unweighted if it includes expenses that are unrelated to individual student need. When a significant amount of funding operates outside the formula, however, inequities typically continue to persist, and the system as a whole becomes less transparent.

  Several WSF systems allocate special education resources outside the formula. While these systems may be able to more tightly manage special education staffing levels, they risk distributing these resources evenly across schools and limiting schools' ability to coherently align general and special education resources to meet overall school needs. Systems should periodically review resources held outside the model and assess their impact on equity, flexibility, and transparency.

  MPS currently allocates $691 million or 73 percent of its total $1.17 billion budget, $946.6 million of which is operations, to school-level allocation based on its WSF.[5] This represents transparent resource use but may or may not allow for flexibility at the school level, depending on how tightly the district maintains control over how these resources are deployed.

- *Do significant restrictions on the uses of per-pupil funding allocations exist?* As argued above, if mandates require that schools spend a certain amount of their allocated per-pupil funding on specific staff positions or service models, school leaders are unable to exercise the type of flexibility that weighted student funding intends. Restrictions typically come from state and federal grant funding-use requirements (as in the case of Florida's class-size amendment and revenue stream), collective bargaining provisions (typically around teacher load, release time, and class sizes), and within-district policy.

School districts should consider what types of funding restrictions they have in place and how existing restrictions limit the school-level flexibility needed to reallocate dollars where they are most needed. This is most challenging for districts with low overall funding levels and a high degree of restriction coming from collective-bargaining agreements and state law.

- *Does the district have a lot of small schools that struggle to make efficient use of per-pupil dollars?* Small schools tend to have higher fixed costs and therefore have fewer resources left to implement school designs to match their needs. At the elementary level, for example, size-driven costs increase rapidly on a per-student basis as enrollment falls below 350. Examples of these costs include schools' front-office staffing (e.g., all schools need a full-time principal and secretary). They also include extra homeroom teachers that are needed to comply with class-size maximums (a school with thirty fourth-graders and a class size max of twenty-eight requires two fourth-grade teachers and will operate with a higher cost per student than a larger school that can staff classrooms closer to the class size max) as well as special education resource teacher positions (in Duval County, Florida, elementary schools were allocated resource teachers for K–2 and 3–5 no matter how few students with special needs were in the school).

Districts that are experiencing enrollment declines or that operate older facilities that were designed to serve smaller numbers of students face a difficult choice over how to cost-effectively provide the best education to the greatest number of students: allow small schools to continue to use a large share of resources in nonstrategic ways or take on politically challenging closures or merges and require students to attend schools further from their homes.

- *How much do teacher compensation and quality vary across schools?* Most districts that implement WSF use average salary as a means of charging schools for the teachers they employ. This means that regardless of whether a teacher actually makes $40,000 or $70,000, she costs the school the same amount. If teacher compensation varies greatly across schools due to differences in length of service, the practice of charging average salaries as part of the funding formula will actually drive up inequitable spending.

In addition, weighted student funding does not address variation in teacher quality across schools. Additional measures would be needed to address this particular type of inequity, including the use of incentives (see below and also see Nair, this volume).

MPS and other districts relying on weighted student funding systems, particularly those with a high percentage of small schools, face unique struggles in the face of declining revenue. They must balance the need to give school leaders adequate flexibility, as WSF intends, and also ensure that all schools remain financially viable and offer a minimum level of services to students.[6]

In the end, districts like Milwaukee may use the transparency provided through WSF to demonstrate that schools below a certain size threshold aren't viable without significant subsidy. They can then frame discussions about school closure to be about a quality level of service to all students and not just about saving money.[7] Finally, fully addressing the need for equity in districts like MPS requires that funding levels between it and competing education providers are suitably adjusted for differences in the characteristics and needs of the students served by each. It should also take into account the district's status as the provider of last resort.

Allocating resources to schools equitably, flexibly, and transparently is critical to ensuring that systems are making the most of the resources they have, but doing so does not ensure that schools use their allocations productively. The three most significant opportunities for districts to maximize the effective use of resources are within the areas of teacher compensation, school design, and special education.

TEACHER COMPENSATION

Teacher compensation plays a significant role in shaping a district's funding strategy and human-capital management system: Teacher salaries and benefits now typically account for between 45 and 50 percent of a district's annual costs.[8] MPS is near the national average. According to data from the Wisconsin Department of Public Instruction, the district spends 48 percent of its total budget ($620 million out of $1.28 billion) on salaries and benefits for current teachers.

Between 1970 and 2005, overall spending—adjusted for inflation—essentially doubled from $3,800 to $8,700 per pupil nationwide. Eighty percent of the increase in per-pupil spending has gone toward creating additional staff positions and covering the higher cost of benefits.[9] Adjusted for inflation, teachers' salaries remained essentially flat between 1990 and 2010.[10] The majority of districts' compensation systems are still rooted in structures that have remained unchanged since the 1970s, and continue to build in automatic salary increases that are unrelated to teacher results or contribution. Compensation structures shape the fiscal sustainability of the district's budget and have a significant impact on who enters and remains in the district—and, more broadly, in the teaching profession.

Individual systems (Baltimore City[11]; DC Public Schools[12]; New Haven, Connecticut[13]) across the country are beginning to evolve their compensation systems to better reflect their strategic objectives: to attract and retain high-performers, to leverage highest-performers for continuous improvement, and to create teacher teams and assignments to match school and district performance objectives. These systems are beginning to drive toward a value proposition that recognizes the complexity inherent in teaching and offers advancement opportunities that leverage a teacher's skill set in support of a district's goals and priorities.[14]

Typical urban school districts, however, continue to compensate teachers primarily for longevity and the accumulation of education credits—neither of which is strongly linked to performance or contribution.[15] ERS' analysis of ten urban school districts found that payments for length of service and education credits typically account for more than 80 percent of a teacher's potential career salary increase, while only 10 percent is based on strong job performance or taking on increased responsibility. This disconnect compromises a district's ability to attract and retain top talent[16] and locks a large percentage of funding into expenditures that are not aligned with its instructional mission.

Urban districts seeking to reform their systems must carry out specific analyses in order to thoughtfully reform their compensation systems.

- *How effectively is it measuring teacher effectiveness? How is effectiveness distributed across the workforce?* New compensation systems must be grounded in accurate data on individual effectiveness and contribution. If the system is unable to identify its high performers, then the chances of designing a compensation system to retain or leverage them seems remote. In the absence of a valid measurement system, major compensation changes can be designed, but should not be implemented.
- *How much is it spending on education credits and longevity payments? How are these dollars distributed across the current workforce?* This type of analysis will help the district understand which types of teachers receive a disproportionate amount of compensation via mechanisms that are not aligned with teaching effectiveness and will shed light on the best reform approach.[17] Understanding the nature of this distribution will provide insight on how to best transition from the current compensation system toward a new system based on performance, responsibility, and contribution.

The concentration of a small number of teachers at the high end of the salary schedule, for example, opens up more possibilities for targeted and aggressive reform such as early retirement incentives. In contrast, the compression of a larger share of the teacher workforce at the top step will make redefining the salary schedule more difficult because funding the new system will require either significant reinvestment or a reduction in salary. Unless alternative incentives are made available, it will be difficult to retain high-performing teachers on reduced salaries.

- *How does compensation currently fit into a broader teacher-value proposition?* Compensation is just one piece of a broader set of incentives upon which teachers make career choices. Working conditions, career and growth opportunities, and benefits also play a role. A compensation strategy must take these factors into account. A district with a high degree of variation in principal effectiveness and school working conditions may want to invest more in differentiating compensation levels across schools than a more homogeneous district, for example.

  Districts like MPS must be cognizant of aspects of the value proposition such as job security and benefits that are beyond their direct control. If states or municipalities are reducing benefits and job security for public-sector workers more broadly, the district must adapt its compensation design accordingly.

- *What, then, are the best investments for a district to make in order to meet the compensation objectives described above and achieve its instructional mission?* In a typical district, a reallocation of only 0.2 percent from the operating budget's spending on steps and lanes could free the money needed to provide $10,000 stipends to incentivize the district's best teachers to teach in the high-need schools, for example.[18] Careful examination of current data will allow MPS to decide on the path of least resistance toward a more effective teacher-compensation model.

As with other core aspects of school-system reform, incremental change is unlikely to achieve widespread impact. Full redesign of the value proposition will be necessary in order for districts like MPS to attract, retain, and leverage an excellent teacher workforce over the long term. (For a longer discussion on human-capital management, see Nair, this volume.)

SCHOOL DESIGN

School design addresses how schools can organize their resource allocations based on their instructional models and specific school needs in the most cost-effective way possible. Three important determinants of student outcomes are relevant to school design—teaching effectiveness, the amount and nature of individual attention that students receive, and how instructional time is utilized. Strategic improvements in how time and staff are utilized offer districts like MPS opportunities to achieve significant cost savings and create better learning environments for students in the process. (For a complete discussion and proposed strategies, see Horn and Evans, this volume.)

In studying school-level resource use, we've identified several common misalignments that can be redirected to improve efficiency.

- *Uniform class sizes.* Although class-size mandates historically intended greater individual attention for students, these restrictions often prevent principals from staffing teachers according to student need. Strict class-size requirements force a district to spend money on a greater number of teachers or aides, ignore the district's distribution of teaching effectiveness, and limit the number of students who access high-performing teachers. Districts that are already down a path of accurately evaluating teacher effectiveness can use an incremental increase in class size as means of improving overall teaching effectiveness through performance-based lay-offs. ERS estimates that a typical urban district could free close to 2 percent of its total operating budget by increasing average class size in grades 4–12 by only two students.[19] If this increase occurs in the context of strategic school-design changes, a greater number of students could receive targeted intervention at a lower overall cost to the district.
- *Low class sizes in non-core and advanced areas.* Most districts we study invest in two- to four-student-smaller classes in non-core and electives than in core subjects,[20] despite a strategic focus on English and math. This misalignment results from an effort to offer a full breadth of course offerings to maximize student choice and engagement, combined with conventional course structures.

  In a typical district, increasing secondary non-core class sizes by four students would free up 0.8 percent of the district's total budget.[21] Pooling elementary classes across special subjects at the elementary level, shifting some non-core classes to be single semester and making their teachers itinerant over multiple schools at the middle school level, and exploring nontraditional course offerings (virtual, university/other partnerships) for high schools are examples of cost-reduction techniques for non-core classes that preserve breadth of offering.

In order for MPS and similar urban districts to organize resources in schools effectively—in ways that focus on performance goals and student needs and maximize return on investment—they must rethink the traditional uses of time and staff that hinder student progress. Overall, truly strategic school designs demand more than incremental change around the edges of existing systems. Efforts to improve teaching effectiveness, individual attention, and instructional time must be coordinated to build new structures—strategic school designs—that maximize resources and leverage the full potential of the school day.

SPECIAL EDUCATION

The final area of school-based spending where we see substantial misalignment is in special education. District leaders often treat special education spending as a black box: they are unclear on how it connects to service delivery and wary of realigning resources without triggering compliance violations, costly penalties, or even lawsuits. Ironically, it can be the system's response to regulations and restrictions that compromises the effectiveness of services to the students they intend to protect.

In many systems, reallocating resources away from cost-inefficient practices can enable districts to curtail annual special education spending increases and instead reinvest spending toward improving outcomes for students with disabilities. With spending of $189.4 million on special education, MPS's investment of 27 percent of its operating budget on special education is significantly higher than other urban districts we've studied.[22] Given the magnitude of special education spending, it warrants close scrutiny. We commonly find two areas of inefficiency:

- *Overclassification.* Districts often place an unnecessarily high number of students in special education when general education would be more appropriate. Lack of consistent or high-quality academic interventions for struggling students results in costly special education referrals that could have been avoided. In one district we worked with, identification rates for African American boys in the middle grades were several times the rates of other students. In other districts, state or district funding policies have provided perverse incentives for schools to overclassify students, such as the maintenance of specific staff positions that are directly dependent on the share of classified students.

Classification as special education does not by itself provide the basic instructional elements that students need to be successful—including access to an effective teacher, high expectations, and a rigorous curriculum.[23] Effective and timely instructional differentiation strategies, such as Response to Intervention (RTI), make it easier for teachers to assess and respond to individual student progress and help reduce the incidence of inappropriate referrals.[24]

It should be noted that urban districts with large student populations enrolled in private and charter schools often have above-average classification rates—as district schools typically serve a disproportionate share of special education students relative to other school types. Given the estimate by the School Choice Demonstration Project of the University of Arkansas that somewhere between 7.5 percent and 14.6 percent of Milwaukee voucher pupils are classified as having special needs,[25] this may in fact be contributing to Milwaukee's classification rate of almost 20 percent[26] (relative to a national average of 13.2 percent).[27]

- *Low "fill rates."* Overstaffing is an additional source of inefficiency in special education. Although students with specific types of disabilities often require smaller class sizes, the number of teachers and teaching assistants who staff special education classrooms tends to be higher than the minimum number required by the district or the state. This difference is called the "fill rate"—the minimum number of staff required by staffing ratios divided by the actual number of staff in classrooms.[28] Some urban districts have fill rates as low as 50 percent, meaning they have staffed double the number of teachers and/or TAs that their own guidelines require.

Where districts accurately evaluate teacher effectiveness and have the ability to reduce staffing based on performance, increasing fill rates of special education programs can significantly increase the share of special education students who are taught by effective teachers and reduce costs.[29] Districts with large numbers of small schools, significant enrollment decline (or significant redistribution of enrollment across schools), or policies that strongly promote high-needs special education students being served in their neighborhood school are more likely to have lower fill rates.

Ultimately, the objective of special education is to improve educational outcomes for children with exceptional needs. In order to meet this objective, districts will need to reconsider when and how to spend scarce funding. For example, through capturing increased efficiency on fill rates and bringing special education class sizes from 65 percent to 75 percent, a typical district will save 1.2 percent of its budget. In a district the size of MPS, this would amount to $11.4 million.[30] This funding could be directed to preventative measures such as the expansion of Pre-K and the implementation of an RTI program.[31]

CONCLUSION

Urban systems across the country are facing the double challenge of declining funding and increasing expectations. Many, including Milwaukee, also must compete with charter and other alternative providers for enrollment.

Meeting these challenges will require doing more with less. To this end, systems must look aggressively at how they're using their resources, focusing first on four core areas: school-funding systems, teacher compensation, school design, and special education. In order to reallocate resources more strategically and support improvements in teaching and learning, districts like Milwaukee Public Schools should consider the following action items:

- *Support equity, transparency, and flexibility in the funding system.* When districts such as MPS rely on WSF, they must answer critical questions around equitable weighting of student need, the percentage of funding that runs through the formula, flexibility among school leaders to deploy resources, and whether there is an equal distribution of effective teachers across schools.

Fully addressing the need for equity in districts like MPS requires that funding levels for competing education providers are suitably adjusted for differences in the characteristics and needs of the students served by each and for the district's status as the provider of last resort. Answers to these questions will determine the district's next steps, which may include reducing their number of small, low-performing schools through closure and consolidation and the modification of its portfolio.

- *Structure teacher compensation to recruit, retain, and leverage effective educators.* Accurate information on teaching effectiveness is needed in order for districts to make fair decisions about teacher compensation. This means that establishing a rigorous and reliable evaluation system is typically a district's first step. Districts should then transition away from longevity and education credits as the primary determinants of salary.

A key part of this transition is the district's articulation of its value proposition to teachers, the components of which must be consistent with the district's goals.[32] The shift to a new teacher-compensation system will likely take multiple years, and districts should design the new system in a way that will be financially sustainable.

- *Facilitate a more strategic approach to school design.* Principals, their supervisors, and district leaders should scrutinize whether each school's resources are aligned with its overall academic improvement plan and the district's broader vision for reform. Resources may need to shift toward students with higher needs, which will require moving away from uniform class sizes and redirecting resources toward maximizing individual attention and efficient use of time.

• *Encourage transparency and efficacy in special education spending.* Districts must clearly document, either internally or with the help of an external expert, how exactly special education dollars are spent and work to identify if spending patterns are rooted in mandates or status quo practices. Greater efficiency and quality of service delivery may be achieved through alignment of special education and general education resources.

Systems like Milwaukee must start by assessing current resource use in these targeted areas, quantifying resource misalignments, and identifying barriers to change. Once leaders have a sense of the size of the opportunities and how they connect to an overall reform strategy, they can prioritize realignments based on ease, cost, and impact.

NOTES

1. Education Resource Strategies, "Seven Strategies for District Transformation," 2010, http://erstrategies.org/documents/pdf/ers-seven-strategies.pdf (accessed September 1, 2012).

2. Education Resource Strategies, "School Funding Systems: Equity, Transparency, Flexibility," 2010, http://erstrategies.org/documents/pdf/school_funding_systems.pdf (accessed September 1, 2012).

3. Milwaukee Public Schools, www2.milwaukee.k12.wi.us/portal/FY13/Schools_N.pdf (accessed September 1, 2012).

4. Stephen Frank, "Fair Student Funding and Other Reforms: Baltimore's Plan for Equity, Empowerment, Accountability and Improvement," Education Resource Strategies, 2012, http://erstrategies.org/documents/pdf/BaltimoreLessonsLearned.pdf (accessed September 1, 2012).

5. Milwaukee Public Schools, www2.milwaukee.k12.wi.us/portal/FY13/Financial_State ments_N.pdf (accessed October 1, 2012).

6. Seattle and Cincinnati are two examples of districts that recently chose to convert from WSF to a foundation formula that funds a core set of basic services across all schools.

7. Frank, "Fair Student Funding and Other Reforms."

8. Education Resource Strategies 2011–2012 Benchmark Data.

9. Education Resource Strategies Analysis and District Data.

10. U.S. Department of Education, National Center for Education Statistics, Digest of Education Statistics, 2011 (NCES 2012-001), introduction and chapter 2.

11. Stephen Sawchuck, "On Second Try, Baltimore Teachers Ratify Contract," *Education Week,* November 17, 2010, http://blogs.edweek.org/edweek/teacherbeat/2010/11/baltimore_ teachers_ratify_cont.html (accessed September 1, 2012).

12. District of Columbia Public Schools, www.dc.gov/DCPS/impact (accessed September 1, 2012).

13. Stephen Sawchuk, "Contract Yields New Teacher-Evaluation System," *Education Week*, November 16, 2011 (accessed September 1, 2012).

14. Regis Shields and Christopher Lewis, "Rethinking the Value Proposition to Improve Teaching Effectiveness," December 2012 (accessed May 19, 2013).

15. Karen Hawley Miles and Stephen Frank, *The Strategic School: Making the Most of People, Time and Money* (Thousand Oaks, CA: Corwin Press, 2008).

16. Caroline M. Hoxby and Andrew Leigh, "Pulled Away or Pushed Out? Explaining the Decline of Teacher Aptitude in the United States," *American Economic Review* 94 (2004): 236–240.

17. Education Resource Strategies, "Teaching Job: Restructuring for Effectiveness," 2010, http://erstrategies.org/documents/pdf/ERS-Teaching-FINAL.pdf (accessed September 1, 2012).

18. Education Resource Strategies, "School Budget Hold'em," http://holdem.erstools.org/hold-em (accessed September 1, 2012).

19. Education Resource Strategies, "School Budget Hold'em."

20. Core subjects are English, math, social studies, and science (and foreign language at the secondary level).

21. Education Resource Strategies, "School Budget Hold'em."

22. Milwaukee Public Schools, www2.milwaukee.k12.wi.us/portal/FY13/Schools_N.pdf (accessed September 1, 2012).

23. Stephen Frank and Karen Hawley Miles, *Leveraging the Power of Inclusion for All Students: Rethinking Special Education to Drive District Transformation*, Education Resource Strategies, 2011, 6.

24. Ibid.

25. Ibid.

26. Milwaukee Public Schools, www2.milwaukee.k12.wi.us/portal/FY13/Schools_N.pdf (accessed September 1, 2012).

27. U.S. Department of Education, http://eddataexpress.ed.gov/data-element-explorer.cfm/tab/data/deid/5 (accessed September 1, 2012).

28. Frank and Miles, *Leveraging the Power of Inclusion for All Students,* 9.

29. Ibid.

30. Milwaukee Public Schools, www2.milwaukee.k12.wi.us/portal/FY13/Schools_N.pdf (accessed September 1, 2012).

31. Education Resource Strategies, "School Budget Hold'em."

32. Shields and Lewis, "Rethinking the Value Proposition to Improve Teaching Effectiveness."

Chapter Seven

Harnessing Data and Analytics 2.0

Jon Fullerton

The last decade has seen a tremendous rise in the amount of data available for use in managing and monitoring the performance of schools and school systems. The passage of No Child Left Behind (NCLB) resulted in a deluge of testing data on most students, and the slow but steady installation of new information systems has meant that more and more operational data beyond test scores are available electronically.

In order to meet the performance pressures of NCLB, many school systems are embracing "data-driven decision-making" at the school level by implementing various benchmark assessments (such as the Northwest Evaluation Association's Measures of Academic Progress, Acuity Assessments and Scantron's Achievement Series) and ensuring that school staff use defined processes such as those promoted by the Achievement Network or DataWise to guide and differentiate their instructional strategies with students.

While much has been made of the power of data to improve teaching and the performance of individual schools, school systems have been somewhat slower to focus on the power of these new data to better understand and manage overall system performance.[1] Linking data from different operational domains (e.g., human resources and finance) to student achievement data has the potential to transform the management of school systems, allowing school leaders to think critically about how different types of resources are being used in the system and the relation of these resources to outcomes. Unfortunately, because of a general lack of expertise in using data to guide strategy, sensitivity to releasing performance data publicly, and the political unpopularity of using scarce resources on analysis and IT systems, relatively few large agencies have fully tapped the power of the data they have to better manage the performance of their schools.[2]

This is unfortunate. Districts that do not take full advantage of their data are giving up the opportunity to manage strategically and to make timely course corrections. Districts should be using data to identify things like where they get their best teaching recruits, whether students are getting placed with more and less effective teachers in a fair manner, and what the impact is of falling behind in a specific subject or skill on long-term academic outcomes. Without constantly using, analyzing, and questioning their own data, districts will continue to base their strategies on anecdote, inertia, and political pressure.

At the same time as data are becoming theoretically more available for school districts to use, districts themselves are losing their monopoly status, with competition arising from charter schools, voucher programs, online offerings, and even other districts. Therefore, even as we consider the benefits of better use of data, we should make sure not only to focus on current organizational structures (classrooms in schools in districts) but also to consider emerging delivery systems.

Milwaukee is a particularly useful system to consider, as it has a robust competitive environment. Twenty-eight percent of publicly funded students in Milwaukee attend schools completely outside of the Milwaukee Public Schools' control.[3] Primarily, these students attend schools that accept vouchers through the Milwaukee Parental Choice Program. Another 17 percent attend either district or independent charter schools.[4]

We thus must consider the role of data in improving total system performance and outcomes for *all* students, not just outcomes for students who happen to be in traditional district public schools. Three types of information flow are important:

1. Parents, students, and others selecting schools or other educational services need robust information in order to make informed decisions.
2. Agencies providing educational services (school districts, independent schools, charter schools) need specific management data and analytics to improve their strategic decision-making and ongoing management.
3. State and local policy-makers need system-wide information that will allow them to make accountability decisions and reasonable adjustments to current regulations. Providing readily accessible and analyzable data could also allow system participants (district public schools, independent schools, and charters) to learn from one another.

THE DATA PARENTS NEED

Almost half of publicly funded Milwaukee students do not attend "traditional," district-controlled public schools. This is part of a larger trend toward school choice in large urban areas across the country. For instance, 41 percent of students in Washington, DC, attend charter schools, as do almost 20 percent of students in Philadelphia.[5] These numbers actually undercount the amount of choice available to parents, as many school systems allow students significant choice within the district.

The arguments for allowing public school choice, however, generally presuppose that parents have some basis upon which to choose a school. If reliable information is not available, we would expect choice to be most effectively exercised by parents who have the time and social capital needed to capture nonpublic information about the different options available. Other parents with fewer resources will simply need to guess or not participate in choice at all. Unfortunately, as I have argued elsewhere, the amount of information available to parents as they make this critical decision is often pitifully small.[6]

The situation for Wisconsin is something of an exception here and can provide valuable lessons for other geographies implementing school choice. The Wisconsin Department of Public Instruction has created the Wisconsin Information Network for Successful Schools, which provides a relatively robust set of data on a variety of metrics (including academic achievement, student behavior, and program offerings) that can be accessed by any member of the public.[7]

DPI has also begun to produce growth reports for schools that allow parents to get some insight into the academic growth of students in one school relative to others. These measures compare students' academic growth in a school to the "typical" academic growth of students in the state with similar demographic characteristics and prior achievement levels. In addition, Wisconsin has a new school report card that collects (or will collect) not only student achievement levels, but also information on student growth and the post-secondary readiness of students.

In Milwaukee, the situation is even better. To support the choice program, GreatSchools, a national nonprofit that provides information on schools to parents, has created a "School Chooser" guide to help parents make their decisions. The guide is constructed to be user friendly and contains all of the public and private options available to publicly funded students.[8]

That said, Milwaukee and Wisconsin also provide examples of gaps in the data being made available to parents. First, with the exception of the "School Chooser," the data are often provided in formats not easy for beginning users to understand. While there is good comparative information available, much of the information is in a form that will not be usable by parents, who, unless they have a background in using data, may find it hard to navigate or bring meaning to the charts and tables they are presented. Fixing this issue will require a willingness on the part of the state to interpret and highlight what is important in the data for parents, not just make it available.

Second, the data in the first batch of the recently released state report cards focus almost entirely on academics and some college readiness indicators such as ACT scores. While this is probably the core of what most parents hope schools will focus on, many parents will want to know more about specific program offerings, instructional approaches, and the school community in order to make the best match for their child. While both DPI and GreatSchools' "School Chooser" provide some information on non-core academic programs that are available (e.g., music, athletics) such as the number of programs or percent participating, no detail about the offerings is provided other than that the programs exist.

Finally, and perhaps most importantly, the information parents have access to on student achievement and student growth is *inconsistent across schools*. Until recently, independent schools were not required to test their choice students with the Wisconsin state assessment (the Wisconsin Knowledge and Concepts Examination).

In addition, schools are still not required to test or report on nonpublicly funded students. As a result, the information on the achievement and growth levels of independent schools is spotty at best. While some growth data for publicly funded students attending independent schools may be available going forward, for schools that are not entirely Milwaukee Parental Choice Program (MPCP), the level results will be biased (as many to most students are excluded) and growth results might also be biased, if they are available at all.[9] The net result is that parents will only be able to compare parts of private schools to entire individual public schools—undermining the usefulness of the information that is available.

The new state report cards attempt to create a consistent measure across schools, but the lack of availability of growth scores for high school pupils (because they only take the state test once in high school) and the exclusion of private schools enrolling students via vouchers from the report card system make this an improved measure that still falls short of being a comprehensive tool to help parents select schools.

Policy Recommendations

- States that promote school choice should assume the responsibility of providing parents with robust information about schools, including both the academic achievement and growth of their students and additional information and descriptions of program offerings and school approaches to education.
- The above will require states to develop and maintain rich longitudinal data on all schools in the system—including independent schools. In order to allow for fair comparisons, data should be collected on *all* students in participating independent schools.

• States should also ensure that "parent-friendly" reports and tools are available that can help parents sort through the options available. These tools will require leveraging state longitudinal data, but, for reasons of user-friendliness, may not be best operated by state departments of education themselves. States should consider outsourcing these reports to organizations such as GreatSchools with the proven ability to communicate unbiased information simply and clearly.

THE DATA AGENCIES NEED

While parents need certain information in order to choose schools wisely, leadership and managers in public school districts need a largely different set of data in order to manage efficiently. One might think of MPS as a business that needs to deliver and integrate high-quality services (teaching, student support, food services, transportation) from over 10,000 employees to 80,000 students at more than 160 delivery sites (schools). The budget of the operation is proportional to its scale, over $1.2 billion of current expenditures in fiscal year 2011.[10] Most strategic businesses of this complexity and scale would use sophisticated information systems to track delivery, monitor resource usage, and track customer needs, preferences, and buying habits.

Similarly, school systems could and should use data to understand and manage outcomes across their sites. To manage well, systems should be connecting data across functional areas (particularly human resources, student, and financial data) and use this information to identify performance gaps and potential efficiencies, create strategies for closing these gaps and harvesting efficiencies, plot the expected impact of these strategies, and monitor performance against expectations over time. For instance, district leaders should be able to get answers to the following questions:

• What recruitment sources provide the most successful teachers?
• Are some students receiving the district's most effective teachers year after year while others are receiving the least effective year after year? Why?
• Are teachers receiving professional development in areas appropriate to their developmental needs? Do the professional-development opportunities provided to teachers improve their performance?
• What interventions are most cost-effective with which students?
• How do the resources schools receive map onto their relative student needs?
• How is the progress of students, teachers, and schools related to overall system goals and short-term targets?

Unfortunately, most school systems cannot answer, and often cannot even explore, any of these questions. Three barriers typically hold systems back.

First, many district information systems were developed piecemeal to handle day-to-day operations and to fulfill regulatory compliance needs. For many years, even accurately connecting students to teachers was impossible. While this is rapidly changing, integrating this information back to human-resources systems and ultimately to financial systems is still slow going.

For example, despite a new federal mandate that systems report expenditures by school,[11] systems still budget a large number of school-site personnel centrally, making it difficult to know precisely what resources are being utilized at any given school. Likewise, while school systems can accurately report how much Title I[12] money is being spent, they generally cannot trace that money down to the level of individual students. Information systems that accurately report information across departmental silos at the appropriate level of granularity are still a rarity.

Second, even if such systems were in place, most school systems have a shortage of the type of analytic talent needed to take advantage of them. While there are plenty of analysts involved with counting things, ensuring compliance with bureaucratic regulations, and evaluating historical programs, there are very few "data strategists" able to use data in a proactive way to guide strategic decisions and model their implications for operational leadership.[13] Without highly trained and creative staff to shape management questions, monitor leading indicators for desired outcomes, perform forward-looking analyses, and model potential outcomes of different interventions, even the most advanced information systems cannot meaningfully enhance management.

In the private sector, these types of roles abound, but the need for such positions is just beginning to be recognized in education. However, there are some organizations focused on developing such talent inside of educational agencies. This author's own center runs the Strategic Data Project, which places just such analysts into education agencies and provides extensive training both for these new analysts and for existing analysts within the agency.

Education Pioneers has started a new analyst fellowship program. Likewise, the Education Delivery Institute works with state agencies to create "delivery units" staffed with analysts who can create reasoned outcome trajectories and performance-management systems. Finally, the Regional Education Laboratories established by the Department of Education have been given a new focus on helping systems manage and understand their data as opposed to simply providing third-party research. Nevertheless, this type of analytic capacity is still relatively rare in education agencies and often vulnerable to cuts in times of economic distress.[14]

This vulnerability is the result of the third—and perhaps most important—gap preventing the effective use of data within education agencies. In many districts, most senior management members have grown up professionally in a relatively data-free culture. Because neither data nor analysts were available, senior management has never developed the expectation that the strategic questions asked above should be answered with analysis as opposed to anecdote.

Many operational leaders in education have never experienced examples of how analysis can support strategy development and system management on an ongoing basis. As a result, operational and outcome targets for systems are often set unrealistically high or too low, programs are implemented in a manner that makes it impossible to determine their efficacy at a later date, and, in tough budget times, cuts are made with no reference to the efficacy or efficiency of teachers, schools, and departments.

The three gaps above, of course, can serve to reinforce one another. If leadership does have questions, poor data systems and lack of capacity in the system help ensure that they cannot be answered. As a result, leaders may become skeptical of the value of data and analytics at the system level and underinvest, resulting in continued inability to answer questions. The following recommendations are intended to help systems break out of this vicious circle.

Policy Recommendations

- Districts should ensure that they have analytic capacity that is capable of going beyond historical and compliance reporting to help shape strategy and management processes. Many districts (even large districts) will find it difficult to fund such new positions at the central office before the analysts have been able to prove their worth.

  As a result, local business communities and philanthropies should urge local education agencies to obtain this type of talent and potentially even provide financial support for these positions for a few years. Business leaders may be able to help districts locally source this talent by lending staff for an extended period of time, helping the district structure positions that would be attractive to graduates of policy and business schools, or leveraging national third-party human-capital providers such as those mentioned above.

- Where existing information systems are insufficient to provide the data needed for effective management, district leaders and the business community should make the case for better management systems and ensure that new systems are developed to provide the management information that system leaders need. For example, all publicly funded students should be included in the state's new statewide student information system (currently in development). This will allow schools and systems to capture historical demographic, performance, and other data on Milwaukee's highly mobile student population, ensuring that critical knowledge about students is not lost every time a student switches school sectors.

• Insofar as states are able to support districts in providing sophisticated information systems, data warehouses, and analytical engines to their districts, they should do so. If they are ultimately able to replace individually purchased district information systems entirely, this could result in substantial savings across the system.

Several states, including Florida and Kentucky, already provide their districts with substantial portions of an information systems infrastructure, and inBloom (funded by the Bill and Melinda Gates Foundation and the Carnegie Foundation) is a new initiative working with states to create the data storage and infrastructure needed to allow districts and other local education agencies the ability to store and use student-level data to individualize student instruction. These are both positive developments that one hopes will expand.

THE DATA POLICY-MAKERS AND THE PUBLIC NEED

As noted above, many metropolitan areas have choice environments evolving that will allow publicly funded students to attend schools not controlled by their geographic school district. Milwaukee, for instance, has a very robust choice environment in that its students can attend independent schools, charter schools, and other districts in addition to MPS. As a result, system leaders and civic leaders need to consider all education providers, not just the district, when developing strategies to improve educational outcomes. Given a choice environment and high mobility between systems, simply relying on a district's internal management data to measure and monitor progress will be insufficient both for districts and for communities as a whole.

Both civic leaders and district leaders will want to know the answers to questions such as:

1. What are the characteristics of students and families who switch into and out of the district? Who is attracted to which schools?
2. How do parent preferences implicitly rank schools—and how does this ranking compare to value-added, level scores, or other "public" measures of school quality? In other words, do parents appear to value school qualities other than academic growth? If so, what do they value?
3. Do any schools seem to have particular success reaching different types of students (controlling for prior achievement)? Do different

types of schools have different levels of post-secondary success with similar students?

4. Do any schools seem to be particularly efficient (in terms of spending and resource allocation) in achieving student growth and success?

Once again, the Wisconsin Department of Instruction provides some guidance to those thinking about how to do this. Over the past years, it has created a moderately robust longitudinal data warehouse and the "Multi-Dimensional Analytic Tool," which allows teachers, school leaders, and administrators to track student growth by characteristic and compare to the rest of the state.

In addition, the School Choice Demonstration Project at the University of Arkansas has recently completed a five-year longitudinal study of Milwaukee's school voucher program, creating over thirty reports with detailed information about many aspects of Milwaukee's education system. Although focused on the question of the impact of school choice, this work provides insights into some of the above questions and, importantly, the data collected through this project might serve as a source for answering additional critical questions beyond the focus of the project.

However, the systems that are being developed today have some important limitations. First, they tend to be primarily student-focused. Much management data are lacking—especially links that would allow analysts to connect student programs to financial data.

Second, confidentiality considerations prevent school and district leaders from having direct access to data from other agencies in the state. As a result, it is hard for one education provider to learn from others and also hard for an agency to trace success or failure as students cross providers. This is a problem in the private sector as well—companies often build their competitive advantage around information asymmetries. However, this is an area where we may want to consider appropriately protected information linking of programs and schools to student performance and outcomes as a social good as opposed to a private good of the individual education providers.

Third, and this is particular to Wisconsin, assessments are given in late fall as opposed to late spring. As a result, instruction and programs occurring during two different school years are effectively mashed together in the growth results. While this may be acceptable when looking at performance at the school level (at least when not looking at the first year of instruction in the school), it is likely to introduce considerable noise into any evaluations of teacher groups or targeted, single-year interventions.

One way to mitigate the first two issues above is through the creation of a research consortium. While the Consortium on Chicago School Research (CCSR) was founded over two decades ago, the idea of research consortia for large districts has been rising in popularity over the last few years, with consortia being created in New York, Los Angeles, Michigan, and the Kansas City area, among others.

These consortia are collections of primarily university-based researchers who work in an ongoing manner with their respective local education agencies to provide rigorous analysis that can inform critical issues that the agency or agencies are facing. In 2009, Melissa Roderick, John Q. Easton, and Penny Bender Sebring described the themes that guide the CCSR's approach:

> (1) Research must be closely connected over time to the core problem facing practitioners and decision-makers; (2) making an impact means researchers must pay careful attention to the process by which people learn, assimilate new information and ideas, internalize that information, and connect it to their own problems of practice; and (3) building capacity [of the system] requires that the role of the researcher shift from outside expert to interactive participant in the building of knowledge of what matters for student success. [15]

Such a consortium acts as a thought partner for its agencies and the public, collecting and maintaining data over time, engaging stakeholders in both the selection of what to study and the findings and interpretations of the results.

A consortium could provide several advantages to Milwaukee and other similar districts with robust choice environments. First, it could work with state and local agencies to assemble and maintain outcome data in a "neutral" space across multiple agencies. With this perspective, it would be able to identify key data gaps for all agencies in the system (and for the state). Second, such a consortium could bring a technical capacity to bear on common educational problems that small agencies (charters and independent schools) cannot. Finally, there are often low levels of trust between school districts, charter schools, and schools that receive vouchers. This is not surprising, as these groups are competing—but it does hamper information sharing. A consortium could provide analyses that are seen as credible by all parties on questions and identified as most important by these parties.

However, creating a consortium will not completely solve the data challenge facing policy-makers and managers in a multi-provider environment. Because a consortium would need to work with many stakeholders and agencies in Milwaukee, it could become mired in the politics of deciding what to study. Second, the timelines of academic researchers rarely match those of agency decision-makers. As a result, while a consortium could answer long-term questions around parent preferences and student success in different types of schools, it would be neither responsive nor quick enough to answer certain "real-time" management questions (such as whether a particular program reduces the number of transfers out of MPS) in a timeframe that would be helpful to current leaders.

Finally, there are logistical and financial barriers to the creation of a consortium in places like Milwaukee and all but the largest cities. Chicago,

New York, and Los Angeles are ideal locations to set up consortia. They have very large student populations that allow for studies to have sufficient statistical power to identify patterns; they have a large number of local research universities that can provide the analytic firepower needed to lead the studies; and they have a strong local funder base that can help support the endeavor in an ongoing manner.

Milwaukee and similar cities may struggle to meet these preconditions. Funding may be a particular challenge as more and more localities attempt to start such consortia, all calling on the same national funders.

Policy Recommendations

- States should provide districts, charters, and other education providers with systems that allow providers to compare their results at relatively high levels of granularity. Ideally, states should be able to use these same systems to gain insight into the cost effectiveness of different providers, the movement of students across providers, and the causes of this movement and its impact on student achievement.
- Markets with multiple providers, such as Milwaukee, should consider establishing a research consortium to allow knowledge about providers to be built up over time and made available to policy-makers and providers. However, there are challenges for all but the largest metropolitan areas. Midsize areas may want to consider banding together with other cities to create consortia with sufficient scale, or states may want to consider creating state-level consortia themselves. Both of these solutions would, however, reduce the focus of the consortium on Milwaukee-specific problems.

CONCLUSION

Data have the potential to be a crucial tool in the improvement of student outcomes. While both the state of Wisconsin and the Milwaukee Public Schools bring significant data assets to the table, building on and leveraging these assets to improve performance will be challenging. Ultimately, Milwaukee and other metropolitan areas need to develop data systems that provide consistent and relevant data to parents, school leaders, system leaders, and policy-makers that can cross the boundaries of multiple providers of educational services. This will give states, school providers, and parents the information they need to manage toward outcomes, as opposed to the simplistic data they currently receive that confirms the failure or success of students long after it is too late to do anything about it.

NOTES

1. Kathryn Parket Boudett and Jennifer Steele, *DataWise in Action: Stories of Schools Using Data to Improve Teaching and Learning* (Cambridge: Harvard Education Press, 2007).

2. See Frederick Hess and Jon Fullerton, "Balanced Scorecards and Management Data," in *A Byte at the Apple: Rethinking Education Data for the Post-NCLB Era* (Washington, DC: Thomas B. Fordham Institute, 2007), 160–185.

3. Includes students attending schools in other districts through Chapter 220 and Open Enrollment. Wisconsin Policy Research Institute, *Milwaukee K–12 Education.*

4. Includes students in both district and independent charters. Wisconsin Policy Research Institute, *Milwaukee K–12 Education.*

5. Washington, DC, data from Office of the State Superintendent of Instruction, "2011/12 Annual Enrollment Audit Overview," March 13, 2012, http://osse.dc.gov/publication/2011-2012-enrollment-audit-overview (accessed May 19, 2013). Philadelphia data from National Alliance of Public Charter Schools, The Public Charter Schools Dashboard 2010/11, http://dashboard.publiccharters.org/dashboard/students/page/mkt/state/PA/year/2011 (accessed May 19, 2013).

6. Jon Fullerton, "The Data Challenge," in *Customized Schooling,* ed. Frederick Hess and Bruno Manno (Cambridge: Harvard Education Press, 2011), 153–172.

7. http://dpi.wi.gov/sig/index.html (accessed May 19, 2013).

8. GreatSchools, "Milwaukee School Chooser: 2012–2013," www.greatschools.org/res/pdf/schoolchooser/GreatSchools_Milwaukee_Chooser_2012-2013_English.pdf (accessed May 19, 2013).

9. Small numbers of MPCP students attending some MPCP schools will make it difficult to isolate a school effect in many value-added models.

10. Milwaukee Public Schools, "2011 Comprehensive Annual Financial Report," (accessed May 19, 2013).

11. For a description of this requirement and some of the data challenges attendant to it, see Ruth Heuer and Stephanie Stullich, *Comparability of State and Local Expenditures Among Schools Within Districts: A Report from the Study of School-Level Expenditures,* prepared for U.S. Department of Education Office of Planning, Evaluation, and Policy Development, 2011.

12. Title I "provides financial assistance to local educational agencies (LEAs) and schools with high numbers or high percentages of children from low-income families to help ensure that all children meet challenging state academic standards." See www2.ed.gov/programs/titleiparta/index.html (May 19, 2013).

13. The term *data strategist* is from Sarah Glover, executive director, Strategic Partnerships at the Harvard Graduate School of Education.

14. Strategic Data Project description available at www.gse.harvard.edu/~pfpie/index.php/sdp (May 19, 2013), Education Pioneers at www.educationpioneers.org (May 19, 2013), U.S. Education Delivery Institute at www.deliveryinstitute.org (May 19, 2013).

15. *The Consortium on Chicago School Research: A New Model for the Role of Research in Supporting Urban School Reform,* the Consortium on Chicago School Research at the University of Chicago Urban Education Institute, 2009.

Chapter Eight

Leading Systemic Reform

Heather Zavadsky

Milwaukee, like many other large urban districts, suffers from chronic low performance. For decades, concern over how to improve school districts, particularly urban districts, has fueled a frenzy of reform solutions, policies, and research studies. While some people claim that nothing has changed in education over the past five decades, the growing number of districts yielding dramatic performance gains proves otherwise. Particularly for districts with great potential, like Milwaukee, successful districts provide a wealth of knowledge about improving education through systemic reform to create coherence and consistency where needed while allowing room for choice and innovation.

Despite growing availability of innovative solutions, it is important to keep in mind one of the biggest lessons learned over time: piecemeal reform will not work. Raising achievement for all student groups beyond one great classroom or school requires changing the way we think about education reform. Rather than focusing on a single school level, program, practice, technology, or model, we must focus on desired outcomes and build the system accordingly. This concept falls much in line with the way Michael Horn and Meg Evans (this volume) describe nurturing innovation by providing flexibility, with inputs to be directed toward an explicit set of target outcomes.

This lesson is particularly important, and difficult to heed, in a choice environment as complex as Milwaukee's. In 2012, about 36 percent of Milwaukee K–12 education students attend school outside MPS. The vast majority are doing so with public dollars. Continuing trends suggest that the percentage of Milwaukee students in MPS will continue to shrink. However, over 85,000 students still occupy MPS classrooms, and the district, no matter how many students it serves, remains a crucial piece of the education reform puzzle in Milwaukee. Its importance is highlighted by individual success stories such as Rufus King, Reagan and Carmen high schools, Garland Elementary, and the many other traditional, specialty, and charter schools within the system.

Still, successes are too few and too often confined to schools with selective admission requirements. Comprehensive education reform in Milwaukee means improving options outside MPS, but also identifying the educational values, outcomes, and inputs needed to improve MPS's position as a quality member of Milwaukee's education marketplace.

A strategy for MPS can and should mirror the strategies recommended for non-MPS options. This includes identification of tools and supports, a process for obtaining and developing the right talent as outlined by Ranjit Nair (this volume) and Doug Lemov (this volume), putting in place accountability and monitoring structures to gauge progress as described by Jon Fullerton (this volume), and building quality-control mechanisms such as those described by Mike Petrilli (this volume).

Whether a strategy includes employing differentiated teacher-compensation strategies or partnering with a charter-management organization, the actors and stakeholders should be clear about expected outcomes, organizational beliefs, tools, and supports and about how they contribute to successive progression toward target outcomes. Maintaining coherence for students and families—the consumers—while making room for innovation is important. A "one-size-fits-all" solution is not the answer, but neither is complete decentralization.

MPS has shown a willingness to embrace nontraditional approaches. In 2012, 8 percent of MPS's total enrollment is in charter, contract, and partnership schools staffed by non-MPS employees. These schools operate as independent institutions under contract with the district. Notably, the percentage of MPS students in these classrooms has been capped by a memo of understanding between MPS and the Milwaukee Teacher's Education Association at 8 percent of total enrollment. However, the passage of Wisconsin's collective bargaining reform will enable the MPS board to further embrace these options. MPS has a newfound potential to create an appropriate balance, focused on improvement, in the ways it delivers education to Milwaukee students.

As the examples in the chapter show, creating a successful and sustainable improvement process can be achieved systemically by using the school district as the hub to ensure that focus and support are always front and center. Thus, the district role becomes facilitating development of clear and executable goals and a plan, identifying the necessary inputs, providing implementation support, and assisting with evaluation and course adjustment. Coherence is extremely important for Milwaukee, as it is employing a number of school options and interventions to address performance.

Another way to frame the district's role is that of quality control, as described by Petrilli as regulating certain aspects of inputs and processes; providing outcome-based accountability mechanisms; and broadening opportunities for different types of models and schools to create market-based options for students and parents. MPS can exercise quality control in its traditional role as manager, but can also serve as an increasingly active school authorizer and contractor. The goal is to be creative in delivery systems and acquisition of proper inputs like strong talent and high-leverage resource-allocation practices, but tight on outcomes and certain processes to ensure alignment and transparency for consumers.

Creativity and systems are typically at odds, yet both can be accomplished simultaneously and well. This chapter will draw upon lessons learned from high-improving and award-winning urban districts such as Aldine, Texas; Boston; Charlotte-Mecklenburg, North Carolina; Denver; and Garden Grove, Long Beach, and Sacramento, California, all of which have created conditions to yield marked improvement in student achievement, particularly in the most struggling schools. These districts were selected based on their ability to raise student achievement while improving various aspects of their overall systems. Information from the districts largely came from interviews with superintendents, associate superintendents, and deputy superintendents.

The following sections will provide a simple framework through field-based examples of how to organize a coherent systemic reform approach while juggling the many other contextual factors that can impede progress. The framework provides steps and examples that apply to three phases of reform work:

- assessing and planning,
- implementing, and
- evaluating and revising.

The chapter will conclude with a summation of lessons from high-improving districts.

ASSESSING AND PLANNING

The first phase for a good improvement strategy is to identify desired outcomes for the system, assess its current status, and map out a plan to obtain desired outcomes. While seemingly simple, the process can be quite complex and time-consuming. Among barriers to improved outcomes are long-term institutional culture, limiting policies at all levels, entrenched beliefs about education and expectations, and societal realities.

Districts that are known for having achieved wide-spread improvement, particularly those facing challenging conditions, spend considerable time on this phase to get the right people at the table, create an appropriate plan based on what works, gain buy-in, and prepare the many intricate parts of the system that need to fall into place. Milwaukee's long history of contested and often-failed plans for improvement illustrates what happens when reforms are produced without buy-in of both the community and a significant number of non-MPS education providers. The steps to beginning the process are to identify a reasonable number of short-term and long-term outcome goals, clarify beliefs about what constitutes high-quality instruction, assess the gap between the current system and those outcomes, and then build a strategic plan to get there.

Assessing—Getting Started

When a superintendent first takes the helm of a district, he or she faces the daunting task of figuring out where to start and what to do. Some will opt to put into place what they implemented in a prior district, which may or may not be similar in context and may or may not be an improvement over the existing practice.

Often with this approach, not much front-end assessing occurs. The trouble with transplanting prior practices is that they may not be viable in different systems, likely will not gain buy-in, and often seed a starting-and-stopping reform regime that changes with each new district leader. [1] There is little evidence that this approach works; it should be avoided without more thoughtful preparation.

Before stepping in and implementing a plan, many leaders engage in a thorough system assessment during what is commonly known in schools as "the first hundred days." Denver superintendent Tom Boasberg, who started in 2009, helped improve numerous struggling schools through innovative programs and charter partnerships. Rather than coming in as a new leader and changing the entire system, Boasberg spent the first hundred days to nine months observing in schools, meeting with his cabinet, and speaking to numerous stakeholders to assess what was working, identify areas of tension, and understand the culture and climate. Next, he and his team spent time analyzing multiple data sources, including achievement data, student surveys, enrollment trends, and discipline data to inform the district's top priorities.

In 2009, Sacramento superintendent Jonathan Raymond inherited a district that he felt had many issues, from poor academic performance to unacceptable school facilities. Raymond was able to improve overall academics and school conditions across the district and yield performance increases in six out of seven targeted turnaround schools.

Like Boasberg, Raymond spent his first hundred days speaking to people, observing in classrooms, and reviewing data. While Boasberg found many viable structures and practices in place, Raymond found virtually none. Thus, he reorganized his central office team to support and connect instruction-related departments, provided closer oversight to schools, and targeted improving teaching through the use of data inquiry methods.

In contrast, Chris Steinhauser, a product and long-term veteran of Long Beach, had worked side-by-side with the previous superintendent of ten years, Carl Cohen, when he inherited the district. Consequently, Steinhauser already knew the culture of the district and had seen the reform work ten years prior. Thus, Steinhauser focused on how he could accelerate what was already started by moving the improvement process down from the secondary to the elementary level. The important commonality among these three leaders is their decision to wait until they understood system conditions before deciding what to execute and how.

Creating a Strategic Plan

Once district leaders understand current conditions and target outcomes, they need to build a clear strategic plan, with a framework for measuring progress, to identify the tools and strategies necessary to get there. This activity is similar to what Kingsland (this volume) describes in what he calls "Design Principal One" for creating a recovery school district. District leaders believe that a concise, thoughtful, and manageable strategic plan is imperative for clearly articulating goals and strategies; identifying the components that must connect and align; creating accountability for implementation; and maintaining focus.

Many examples of strong strategic plans can found on the Web.[2] The Denver 2010 Plan outlines in detail how to address such essential elements as the instructional core, human capital, family and community engagement, strategic financial resource management, and expectations for accountability. Aside from the content itself, the biggest issues in building a solid strategic plan are deciding whom to involve during the process, determining a reasonable number of goals or reform strategies, identifying the inputs that must connect and align for execution, and ensuring that system actors follow it.

Many districts find that gaining buy-in and leveraging expertise in the crafting of a strategic plan can become an extensive and time-consuming process. However, many leaders attest that it is worth the time and effort. To make sure their plan sets the right targets and gains buy-in, Long Beach leaders spend significant time building their plan with multiple stakeholders representing all aspects of the system.

For their latest strategic plan, sixty-five people met for six months working on mission, vision, values, and metrics. District leaders note that the

planning team always includes two board members through the entire process to maintain board buy-in. In most districts, as in Long Beach, the plan
covers a five-year time span. While the process may seem daunting, Long
Beach leaders feel the end result is thorough and thoughtful and results in
widespread adoption.

Because a strategic plan should have a manageable number of focus
areas—three to five according to most of the superintendents interviewed—
leaders must consider how to identify and prioritize what will be accomplished in a given year. Long Beach began its improvement process many
years ago by addressing three specific initiatives: adopting school uniforms
to set a cultural change toward academic rigor, requiring summer school for
third-graders reading below grade level, and ending social promotion.

Even though three is a small number of initiatives, Steinhauser emphasized the importance of understanding how many components must connect
to implement or improve in these three areas. For example, to end social
promotion, the district had to change professional development, realign the
work of the research department, and find appropriate assessments and interventions. According to Steinhauser, "All of these things change the culture of
the system, as does having positive results and making sure you aren't just
shooting random arrows. You can't say you are working on 'x' and then
bring in 10 other unrelated things; nothing will get accomplished." Other
leaders confirmed that losing focus can quickly foster a "this-too-shall-pass"
culture within the district.

Along with limiting the number of goals and initiatives, the focus for the
plan should be on teaching and learning or "what hits closest to the classroom," in the words of several leaders. For Laura Schwalm, superintendent
of Garden Grove Unified School District since 1999, that means building the
instructional capacity of teachers, setting common expectations, and addressing aspects of the system that most impact kids: "If it's the bus schedule and
kids are showing up late, then that has to be addressed."

Another good place to start, according to Schwalm, is to "figure out what
is driving your people the craziest and fix that; it will raise your credibility
and allow you to move the rest of your plan forward." The district, near
Anaheim, California, won a prestigious Broad Prize for Urban Education in
2004.

Using an articulation of beliefs and theory of action is helpful for illustrating how the goals and strategies connect systemically. All too often, district
strategic plans consist of what feels like a random list of goals. To help
communicate how their goals and strategies relate, Denver leaders use a
graphic to illustrate how the pieces fit together (see figure 8.1). Taken from
the 2010 Denver Plan, the graphic depicts the various micro-system levels
moving from the inside out, showing first classrooms (students, content, and

teachers), schools (people, resources, family, and community), and culture (service and high expectations) as a means to tie together the system.

Figure 8.2 illustrates the key focus areas for Charlotte's 2014 plan. While it does not show relationships, it does illustrate how all activities fall under two main focus areas: improving teaching and managing performance. Included in the graphic are specific measurement goals for each delineated strategy.

The important part of the actual strategic-plan document is that it clearly delineates target goals, mission vision, and beliefs, and it illustrates to various system actors and consumers how all the pieces connect toward achievement of desired outcomes. Additionally, it addresses how all of the essential inputs—curriculum and instruction, human capital, performance manage-

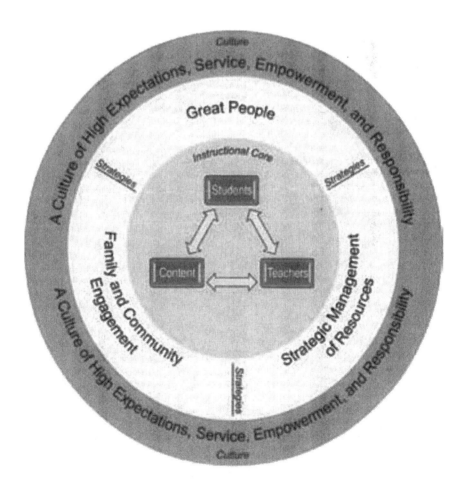

Figure 8.1. 2010 Denver Plan Framework. Used with permission from Denver Public Schools.

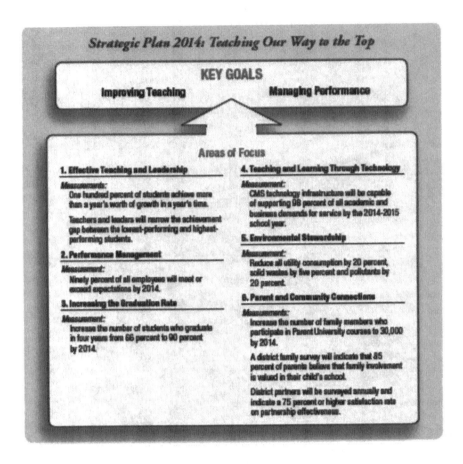

Figure 8.2. Charlotte-Mecklenburg 2014 Strategic Plan Framework. Used with permission from Charlotte-Mecklenburg Schools.

ment or accountability, interventions, and stakeholder relationships—will be addressed.

Milwaukee has almost every one of these elements present in its current strategic plan, which was implemented in 2007 and runs through 2012. Goals, objectives, outcome measures, mission/vision/beliefs, and action steps are clearly delineated.[3] However, the strategic plan is virtually absent from public discourse and has received almost no media attention.

The development of MPS's next plan, the first under the leadership of Superintendent Gregory Thornton, must clearly articulate where flexibility can be granted, and delineate structures and practices that can better connect the right aspects of the system for tighter alignment and coherence. In addition, work should be done to make the plan highly visible, measurable, frequently referenced, and accessible to relevant stakeholders. Including feedback from teachers and principals would also be a useful step for the district, as there seems to be some communication and buy-in gaps between schools and central office, as evidenced by results from a teacher survey conducted by the University of Chicago.[4]

IMPLEMENTING

Once a strategic plan is in place, a step that straddles planning and implementation must first occur: organizing for implementation. This means considering organizational structures across the central office, across and among schools, between the central office and schools, and with various levels of stakeholders. In addition to structures, priming for implementation might also entail setting procedures to allow for open and accessible communication.

The goal is to ensure that all parts of the system—classrooms, schools, and central office—have the right tools and support to maintain consistency and alignment. For example, using pay-for-performance compensation structures to attract and retain teachers requires not only involvement from human resources but also involvement from payroll, principals, and teachers, as well as adequate data systems, accurate evaluation and measurement tools, and media and communication strategies. How the various structures and processes are set up to work in concert to execute the plan is a crucial step for implementation.

Once in place, implementation should focus on providing support and maintaining coherence and focus for the activities outlined in the strategic plan. Though an MPS strategic plan cannot govern the actions of other education sectors in Milwaukee, its implementation should reflect the reality of a divided marketplace where parents frequently switch not only schools but also sectors. Collaboration between the district and private and charter schools should be pursued where possible to find common ways to further the unifying goal of a higher-performing K–12 education system.

Organizing for Governance and Support

Leaders of high-improving districts often point out the difference between moving into a system with viable existing structures like Aldine, Garden Grove, Boston, Long Beach, Charlotte-Mecklenburg, and, for the most part, Denver, as opposed to one with either too many layers or too many areas operating in silos. For example, when he came to Sacramento, Raymond found no workable structures in place to fully support academics. No academic team existed, there was no logic to how school oversight was organized, and there were no organized efforts to oversee or support teaching and learning. Departments like curriculum, professional development, and human resources all worked separately.

Subsequently, prior to creating a strategic plan, Raymond first created an entire academic division, an accountability division, and a family and community engagement division to better align the work. With many positions in the central office vacant, he had great hiring opportunities, so he focused on tapping talent within the district. He hired a chief academic officer and a technology director, and he assigned three assistant superintendents to oversee schools. He also reorganized the schools from discrete levels (elementary, middle, and high schools) to K–12 geographic areas like feeder patterns, which allowed better coherence and alignment among elementary, middle, and high schools.

In Boston, Chris Coxon, deputy superintendent for teaching and learning from 2001 to 2007 under Tom Payzant, felt that changing the existing central-office structures would not work for him or for the district, so he changed how existing positions were used. For example, he moved subject-area instructional coaches and professional-development leaders from the curriculum department to report directly to him. He also moved a high school redesign office to the same department as the high school supervisors to reduce reporting confusion and create better alignment.

Similarly, in Charlotte, Peter Gorman, superintendent from 2006 to 2011, changed the work of his accountability division by having it focus on the effectiveness of all district employees rather than just on student outcomes. Gorman says that it was easier for him to focus on instruction and human-capital development because he was working with experienced finance and operational personnel who kept those areas of the district running smoothly without his intervention.

In addition to organizing the central office, districts must consider the layers and oversight between the central office and schools. For Garden Grove, Laura Schwalm always felt that the district should have a simple, "relatively flat" organizational structure with only one layer between schools and the superintendent. To keep reporting simple so that people would know "how to get things done," she focused on organizing the central office to serve schools, rather than the converse.

In 2004, during Broad Prize interviews, Schwalm had a lean cabinet, with members who could undoubtedly step into each other's positions at any time because they were so well aligned. By design she has always had just two assistant superintendents who provide school oversight and evaluation support to schools, one over elementary and one over secondary. "The downside," explained Schwalm "is those people are very busy supervising up to 47 principals." However, the schools' leaders have said that they benefit from the consistency and simplicity of that arrangement.

While Boasberg kept the reform direction and curriculum the same when he came to Denver, he did make some organizational changes by creating more direct supervision over schools and reducing layers between central office and schools by placing separate supervisors over elementary and secondary schools. Additionally, he hired an executive director over the Office of School Reform and Innovation. This reduced the layers between schools and the superintendent from four to two and created more opportunities for school personnel to interface with him.

Another organizational structure to consider is how to keep different types of school models like charters or virtual schools connected within the district system. In Denver, the district is implementing two large regional turnaround strategies. One, the Far Northeast Regional Effort, is overseen jointly by the district and an external partner, Blueprint Schools, and it engages with high-performing charter-management organizations that share buildings with regular district schools.

These efforts are coordinated in the district by having a central-office leader working closely with the external partner and schools, and through additional support from the Office of School Reform and Innovation. To add more coherence, the district monitors the progress of all schools, even charter schools, through the same accountability framework, detailed further in the "Evaluating and Revising" section below. Thus, Denver students reap the benefits of program alignment as they move from traditional to innovative school models, and the different school models benefit from sharing of facilities, services, and knowledge.

Maintaining Clarity and Coherence

Ensuring that a plan is used to maintain focus and clarity means being thoughtful about creating uniform messages and creating opportunities for structured collaboration that will bring together all the right departments and actors for any given strategy. Much reform fails because leaders do not consider all of the elements that must align, do not create a consistent message, and/or do not create mechanisms for cross-functional work.

To maintain an aligned vision in Boston, Tom Payzant was highly involved in the instructional program, and he insisted on being well informed about curriculum and changes in state standards. He worked hard to keep the district "on message" through frequent meetings with cross-functional central-office teams representing both the operational and instructional divisions. Payzant also excelled at keeping the vision a daily presence.

Coxon related that Payzant would frame everything in the context of the district's reform. "Even if your question has nothing to do with teaching and learning, he will begin talking about the school system, and how schools are not individual islands, there are certain standard practices, all to frame how we think and talk, and then he shows how your question fits. Even if you were looking for quick sound bites, you had to hear the whole 'spiel,' but when you got it, it made sense, and you understood how he was thinking."

In Charlotte, Gorman worked to ensure that the chief finance officer and the chief academic officer were "rowing together in the same direction" to align finance and instruction. He also found monthly meetings between principals and the executive district leaders to be very valuable. In those meetings, Gorman would "connect the dots for them, talk about something related to strategic plan, and then link to upcoming work."

To connect to a broader audience, he would also have a weekly media briefing, particularly when rolling out a new policy, program, or initiative. He also convened "calibration meetings" to talk about how the district handles certain things to create consistency. For example, he would have the principals all bring in their assistant-principal evaluations, talk about them, and compare ratings to discuss how they were evaluating them. Gorman felt it was important to constantly calibrate in various different areas, from instruction to facility management.

In Denver, the central-office departments meet weekly for several hours as an entire team to talk about alignment and academics with an instructional focus. Then teams break down into their specific areas and meet for several hours and report back. Additionally, the assistant superintendent of post-secondary readiness, Antwan Wilson, has his direct reports provide weekly written status reports to provide updates and identify concerns. During the week he meets with each of them individually (there are five) for more substantive discussions.

Balancing Coherence with Choice and Innovation

Coherent systems provide programmatic alignment for students through and across grade-level and school transitions, and they help organize monitoring, support, and evaluation systems to monitor progress. Coherence can be maintained without managing inputs and processes too tightly and without instituting a one-size-fits-all model.

A district can balance oversight in some areas, such as instructional practices and accountability systems, to maintain quality and gauge progress (see Kingsland, this volume, and Petrilli, this volume), yet still provide flexible delivery and model options. MPS has shown a willingness to terminate charter contracts, and, according to the School Choice Demonstration Project, close down schools that were underperforming.[5] The district should continue to make school closure and reorganization decisions based on performance.

In Long Beach, school placement is driven by regional choice rather than by assignment or feeder pattern. When a newly appointed principal took on a chronically low-performing school, he decided to create a middle school arts academy based on what he knew about the students and community. Similarly, Denver schools are also driven by regional choice starting in middle school. Thus, every year in the spring, middle schools begin to "market" themselves to prospective students and parents. In addition to marketing for school choice, Denver and several other districts with schools in one of the four turnaround models use marketing and rebranding strategies to attract students and teachers into newly created models such as science academies, charter schools, and schools of technology, for example.

The important point from these examples is that these schools were allowed to break out of traditional molds as long as they maintained the district's core instructional values and produced what were deemed as acceptable outcomes. The freedom to develop new models was not the only reform strategy; other district processes such as human-capital strategies, professional development, interventions, resource allocation, and accountability structures were still included to ensure that the models were well-supported and successful.

In Milwaukee, during this phase, it might be important for the district to keep its plan present through consistent and frequent messaging, consider how various programs and models can plug into the plan, ensure that parents and community members are well-informed about various school options within the district, and consider what district elements and practices should be centralized and/or supported by the district to maintain educational coherence for students as they transition through the K–12 continuum.

EVALUATING AND REVISING

The one thing all high-improving districts have in common is a strong performance-management system. One of the discoveries that struggling districts often make is a lack of meaningful or timely data. The ability to make course corrections at all levels before small problems become bigger is paramount to the improvement process. As Jon Fullerton asserts in his piece on research and development, many district leaders believe that they have reams of data, but in reality, they are "data rich and information poor."

Being data-driven means more than collecting data; it means having a powerful data-management system, useful assessments that reflect what was taught and learned, structured monitoring systems and tools, time to review and discuss data, and knowledge about how to interpret and respond to data. Despite the fact that MPS has been a pioneer in the use of value-added data, there is little evidence that this information is being consistently used to guide decision-making at the school or district level. It is important that the district build a culture that trusts the data and how they will be used.

Powerful Data Systems

The better the data, the more utility they have. For data to be useful to a district, they need to be accessible, easily queried and disaggregated, and, ideally, pulled from multiple sources. The best data systems are those that allow users to review formative and summative assessment results; see student record information like transcripts, absences, and disciplinary infractions; and connect to the curriculum or standards.

One example of a useful and comprehensive data system can be found in Boston. Their system, My BPS, is a "one-stop" system that ties various data sources to instruction, including formative and summative student assessment data, student record data, tips on how to use and interpret the data, links to state standards and learning objectives tied to assessment questions, and samples of exemplary student-written compositions and scores. Interactive graphs displaying student performance data linked to specific questions on state assessments are also available.

The more data sources housed in one system, the better for targeting appropriate interventions. A unique challenge to Milwaukee is the absence of easily accessible performance data across sectors. A single database with information for all Milwaukee pupils that provides a complete data record regardless of school transfers between sectors is crucial for making specific district interventions successful.

Monitoring Strategies

In addition to providing an accessible, comprehensive data system, the district plays a key role in creating continuous monitoring systems to ensure that all levels are implementing the strategic plan with fidelity, and to identify support and intervention needs. While many of these monitoring systems also serve as accountability tools (see below and Petrilli, this volume), classroom-monitoring systems often come in the form of structured walk-through processes. Walk-throughs differ from typical classroom observations, as they are often implemented separately from teacher evaluations and are structured to observe certain aspects of instruction. High-improving systems commonly implement structured walk-through processes with a team composed of leaders and teachers who use a rubric to document specific target activities, such as using appropriate questioning techniques. Boston implemented quarterly curriculum-monitoring walk-throughs to ensure that the target standards and their selected instructional strategies were being implemented. To provide flexibility, Boston required fewer adherences to those structures in high-performing schools and focused more closely on struggling schools. In addition to walk-throughs, districts also monitor implementation of the plan through the collaborative meetings described earlier under the "Implementing" section.

To provide timely instructional information at the school level, high-improving districts implement formative assessments, typically on a quarterly basis, if not even more frequently. The key to these assessments is that they are aligned with what was taught and provide diagnostic information on targeted learning objectives. In addition to using released state assessment items and teacher-developed assessments, Garden Grove contracted with professional test writers who produced the assessments based on blueprints provided by teachers to ensure the end product was valid, was aligned, and provided a good diagnostic.

Aldine, a past Broad Prize winner from Texas, gave students common and benchmark assessments anywhere from every three to six weeks to ensure that students were mastering learning objectives and to regroup and match student needs (even at the elementary level) to teacher strengths. The key criterion for formative assessments is that they measure mastery of what is taught and are designed to meet students' instructional needs as early as possible, rather than waiting until intervention needs become greater and more drastic.

Accountability Systems and Tools

Having scads of data sources is not useful without a mechanism or tool to examine the data holistically to gain a complete picture of system-wide progress. Many high-improving districts have several accountability tools for this purpose, including their strategic plan. In Charlotte, each line item in the strategic plan includes a due date and assigns a person responsible for managing the task and reporting progress regularly. Additionally, the plan is revisited twice a year through executive team retreats and quarterly board updates, and it is used as a central-office evaluation (as was the case in several other districts).

Similarly, Boston's Whole School Improvement Plan includes formative and summative assessment data tied to school goals that feed into the district's goals. Garden Grove monitors school performance through the Single School Plan, which utilizes formative and summative data along with data from Action Walks to measure progress toward school and district goals.

In addition to the strategic plan, some districts create another accountability tool. Aldine uses a Baldrige-based scorecard that includes formative, summative, and walk-through results that directly feed into action plans.[6] Scorecards have been implemented at the classroom, grade, feeder-pattern, and district levels. Similarly, Denver leaders created their own accountability tool to gain more nuanced information about school performance. The Denver School Performance Framework provides a color-coded rating that results from the examination of assessment data (both proficiency and growth), college readiness, student surveys, discipline, and much more. Denver leaders believe that all of those metrics help the system actors think more broadly about the many variables that impact student achievement, attributed to both the students and the systems. District leaders also receive an outside diagnostic that provides more information on academic performance, the learning environment, and organizational effectiveness of both schools and the district. If an intervention is potentially needed in Denver, the district also begins a community-engagement process after there is internal engagement at the target schools.

The important aspect of having comprehensive monitoring and accountability tools and processes is to be proactive and to use prevention as the main intervention. It will be important that Milwaukee have all these elements in place to ensure that support can be provided proactively and to help diagnose triggers that might impede student success across various system levels.

CHALLENGES

The education improvement process comes with many barriers and challenges, and it hinges upon the ability to obtain the right resources and flexibility to use people, time, and money as needed. Below is a brief summary of barriers related to policy challenges, fiscal constraints, and stakeholder opposition.

Policy Challenges

Policy challenges are well addressed by the other contributors in this volume, and they should be considered when endeavoring to pursue broader, more sustainable education reform. Denver would not be as successful with its charter partnership strategy without a charter-supportive state. For more information on how to spark policy that will support innovation, see the accompanying pieces written by Michael Horn and Meg Evans on innovative models and Neerav Kingsland on creating a recovery district. An additional state-level issue is the availability of accessible and useful data for districts. To read more on strengthening policy in this area, see Jon Fullerton's piece on research and development (this volume).

Fiscal Challenges

In 2010, many districts started getting hit in the pocketbook by our country's recession, forcing them to make tough decisions about what they funded and resource allocation in general. For concrete information on how districts can better align resources to their goals and strategies, see the piece authored by Jonathan Travers, Genevieve Green, and Karen Hawley Miles (this volume).

In addition to the strategies they propose, many high-performing districts note that working to be more aligned and coherent is also an important fiscal practice, as is using this purchase approval question to system stakeholders: "How does this purchase relate to district and school goals?" Given the ongoing loss of students that MPS is experiencing, district reform strategies must be based on realistic enrollment and budget forecasts. Wherever possible, cross-sector collaboration should be pursued so that shared costs such as data systems can be borne by multiple sectors.

Stakeholder Opposition—Unions

When dealing with stakeholder opposition, many leaders had similar advice: keep stakeholders continuously involved and informed, particularly at key decision points, to offset opposition and gain buy-in early. While most leaders know this, they need to be sure to take the time to do it, and in a genuine and well-structured manner that makes good use of others' time and expertise.

There are few barriers that impact the ability to use people, time, and money as much as restrictive teacher-union contracts. In Sacramento, to protect the district's investment in Priority School teachers (improvement schools), the district leveraged a provision in the education code that allows leaders to waive seniority-based layoffs for teachers with unique skills, competency, and training. District leaders were very intentional about the training and support their Priority School teachers received, which they meticulously documented.

It is important, according to Superintendent Jonathan Raymond, to leverage available tools to protect "the most vulnerable students." To date, this strategy has been successful. However, the local teachers union supported by the California Teachers Association has filed a lawsuit trying to remove this provision from the California Education Code.

Chris Steinhauser in Long Beach also had his share of union obstacles, but he overcame them by making sure he read the entire union contract, even as a principal. "Subsequently," he recounted, "I never had a grievance. I knew what I could do, and when someone would complain, I'd refer them to the contract." When he opened up advanced-placement classes for all students (requiring more training for teachers and a host of other changes), he said teachers were livid. However, the contract allowed him to do it.

According to Steinhauser, leaders frequently hide behind contracts and policies rather than moving forward on something that is difficult to do. He saw that behavior as problematic because "the superintendent has to be willing to be fired. Not do anything illegal, but willing to be fired and stand up for what's right for kids. It's critical; it's not about ego; it's about what's right for kids."

Collective-bargaining reform has made union opposition less of a challenge in Milwaukee than it was in years prior. The district's willingness to make aggressive fiscal reforms that go into effect at the conclusion of the current MPS-MTEA union contract suggest that the district is willing to unilaterally take actions unpopular with organized labor. Still, collaboration and consultation with organized labor are important so that staff members have the necessary buy-in for—and willingness to execute—reforms enabled by Act 10.

Stakeholder Opposition—Community

Nothing attracts people to schools and community meetings faster than when schools enter into turnaround, reconstitution, or closure. The recent failed attempt at a mayoral takeover of MPS demonstrated that reform efforts, no matter how well meaning, will be derailed if they move further than the public's willingness to reform. In Denver, for example, when asked about how to deal with community pushback against school closures and charter schools, district leader Antwan Wilson stated, "You have to be committed to prolonged community processes to address their doubts and concerns."

One problem with the community-engagement process cited by Wilson was that often stakeholders believe the meetings are just a placating process and that district officials have already made up their minds. Wilson emphasizes the importance of being committed to conversations and processes that offer opportunities to alleviate those doubts and to take those opportunities to let people know that you genuinely want their input. In addition to community meetings, he cites the importance of inviting stakeholders to come in and see schools, and helping them understand that the district is "trying to deliver what we promised."

While the leaders all agreed that preemptive tactics such as reading contracts, gathering evidence, and conducting stakeholder meetings can be time-consuming, they all felt it was worth it on the front end, because it avoids longer delays or having to completely redo work in the end. Steinhauser affirmed, "You need to take the correct steps and get the proper stakeholders involved. When I get in a hurry and skip those steps, we end up having to go back. It takes time and I'm impatient, but when I violate those steps I always have to repeat them. It's a big reminder: Learn from history, don't violate it."

Like most urban districts, Milwaukee shares these challenges. One way to address these challenges is to increase communication among and between key stakeholders. This means moving past the debate on market share and moving toward a cross-sector discussion of how to use limited resources to improve K–12 outcomes for students who may attend private, charter, and public schools at different points in their education careers.

Moving from the inside out, school choice does not work well if all parents are uninformed about their choices; parent involvement cannot happen without tight school-parent communication. Teacher buy-in and trust are best nurtured through reciprocal communication that treats them as professionals. Oversight and communication between schools and the central office can become easier and clearer with fewer organizational layers.

The elimination of collective bargaining in the state of Wisconsin represents a significant source of leverage for MPS and other school districts in the state with regard to overcoming many traditional barriers to progress in education. With the role of teachers unions limited to certain aspects of salary and employee grievances, Milwaukee leaders have the opportunity to capitalize on greater flexibility over people and time and to think differently about how to best use these resources.

LESSONS—PUTTING THE PIECES TOGETHER

To supplement the examples within this piece from the three systemic reform phases and challenges, below is a summary of takeaways:

Systemic Reform

Balance oversight and coherence with innovation.

- The district serves as a logical hub for organizing and supporting coherent reform.
- Reform does not need to be one-size-fits-all; ideally it is tight on outcomes and flexible on means, although certain structures and practices are helpful for maintaining coherence.
- Three simple phases of the reform process are assess and plan; implement; and evaluate and review.

Assess and Plan

Identify desired outcomes, assess the current system, and build a plan to reach desired outcomes.

- Take time to observe, query stakeholders, and review multiple data sources before building a strategic plan.
- Use multiple stakeholders in developing the plan and consider illustrating main tenets and theories of action within a decipherable graphic.

- Keep goals few in number and consider the many components that must link up to achieve those goals.
- Use innovative models as just one piece of the system. Include other core elements: curriculum standards and instruction, human-capital plan, performance management, intervention, and stakeholder relationships.

Implement

Organize, support, and monitor alignment and implementation of inputs.

- Minimize layers between the central office and schools to ease reporting and communication processes.
- Facilitate communication among education sectors.
- Focus messages and decision-making on the strategic plan to make it a daily guidepost.
- Create mechanisms to connect the necessary departments and stakeholders to execute the strategic plan. Most district departments have cross-functional commonalities that impact the instructional core.
- Consider how innovative and varied school models can be leveraged and aligned within the district system.

Evaluate and Revise

Monitor progress toward goals and the activities outlined in the strategic plan.

- Put in place powerful data systems that are easy to access and query and that house multiple data sources.
- Provide time to meet and review data at various system levels and adjust strategies as needed.
- Implement frequent monitoring processes like structured walk-throughs to gauge implementation and progress and to support needs.
- Implement frequent formative assessments to provide timely diagnostic information on mastery of what is taught.
- Create an overarching accountability tool to help organize the process of reviewing and responding to data. Include innovative models within the tool.

CONCLUSION

There are many new technologies, models, and tools available to help change how we educate students of all ages. However, leaders must be vigilant to ensure that the adoption of these innovations does not result in isolated, piecemeal reform. While there is no magic formula or playbook for leading successful system-wide reform, there are leaders and districts that offer important lessons that are applicable in most contexts.

Building a clear plan, sticking to and revising the plan, connecting all the appropriate components, addressing a manageable number of levers or activities, focusing on what happens in the classroom, communicating frequently with the right stakeholders, using data continuously to measure progress and identify needs, and staying true to the purpose of providing a high-quality education to all students are the common themes cited by leaders of successful reform approaches. The diversity of what can be called "public education" in Milwaukee presents a particular challenge and opportunity for Milwaukee.

Despite the competition for students, choice, charter, and traditional public schools all share common goals and challenges. Collaboration among sectors should be embraced, not shunned. Two decades of school choice have shown Milwaukee parents to be open to new ideas and innovative approaches to education. A comprehensive strategy containing the attributes listed above can take Milwaukee, and MPS specifically, past experimentation and toward success.

The work needs to be simple in layers and direction, and it needs to be executed with consistency. Additionally, an arsenal of tools and talents must be amassed to offset potential uncontrollable or unconsidered variables that can impede progress. Although difficult, it can be done, as demonstrated by leaders who successfully changed the end game for years to come in their districts.

While there are many obstacles for Milwaukee, the state and district have set in motion a series of actions that can be leveraged to create a new and powerful education system for the district. However, pulling all the pieces together in a complex urban district is difficult. The lessons provided by other urban districts that have made gains through greater systemic coherence could well inform Milwaukee's reform efforts.

NOTES

1. Frederick M. Hess, *Spinning Wheels: The Politics of Urban School Reform* (Washington, DC: Brookings Institution Press, 1998).

2. See http://2010denverplan.dpsk12.org/pdf/Final2010Denver%20Plan.pdf (accessed May 20, 2013) for the Denver plan and www.cms.k12.nc.us/mediaroom/strategicplan2014/Pages/default.aspx (accessed May 20, 2013) for the Charlotte-Mecklenburg plan.

3. To view the 2007–2012 Milwaukee strategic plan, see: www.milwaukee.k12.wi.us/portal/server.../06+District+Strategic+Plan (accessed May 20, 2013).

4. Based on results from Will Howell survey, 2012.

5. Clive Belfield, *Review of the Comprehensive Longitudinal Evaluation of the Milwaukee Parental Choice Program: Summary of Fourth Year Reports* (Boulder, CO: National Education Policy Center, 2011), http://greatlakescenter.org/docs/Think_Twice/TT_Belfield_MilwVouch

er.pdf (accessed May 20, 2013).

6. The Baldrige Education Criteria for Performance Excellence is a tool used to measure an organization's performance in the following key outcome areas: student learning, customer focus, budgetary, financial and marketing, workforce, process effectiveness, and leadership outcomes. For more information, see www.nist.gov/baldrige/about/upload/Measuring_What_Matters_Most.pdf (accessed May 20, 2013).

Conclusion

Putting the Pieces Together

Frederick M. Hess, Carolyn Sattin-Bajaj,
and Taryn Hochleitner

There are many books on how to improve school systems, and all of them are dotted with good ideas. But what they also have in common is a tendency to argue for one change, in policy or practice, as *the* key to school improvement. So, for instance, books will tout new governance systems, new ways to manage teachers, smarter approaches to data, or the importance of better professional development and teacher support. We've much sympathy for all of these ideas.

But, upon reflection, it's inevitably the case that trying to do any of these in isolation reveals something of a Rubik's Cube—changing one piece inevitably means other changes elsewhere. If one steps back and surveys K–12 systems built for a long-ago era of lower expectations and industrial management, the unsurprising truth is that transformational improvement requires not this or that change—but fundamental rethinking. And we believe that the contributors herein provide a blueprint for just that kind of transformation.

In our experience, well-meaning reformers too often settle instead for laying their new proposals atop outdated schools and systems. Even seemingly bold reformers can retain a reflexive attachment to the notion that schooling requires a single teacher in a single classroom of age-graded students. These stubborn routines are as evident in the charter-school sector—ostensibly K–12 schooling's most promising laboratory of innovation—as in traditional school districts.

In this volume, the contributors sketch a bold set of interlocking strategies for dramatically improving the instruction, operations, governance, accountability, talent management, budgeting, and leadership of an entire education-al ecosystem. They dissect the enterprise and name concrete steps that lead-ers—in education, in business, in politics—need to pursue if they are to enable a more fundamental transformation of our schools and systems.

The proposals aren't just complementary; they are *codependent.* Each is most effective when designed and used in tandem. This isn't to say leaders need to simultaneously move on all eight counts in order to be successful, but that these measures will be most impactful when pursued as part of a coher-ent push to comprehensively rethink antiquated structures, regulations, poli-cies, and practices.

PUTTING THE PILLARS TO WORK

At the outset, we introduced each of the pillars—new school delivery, quality control, a recovery school district, professional development, human-capital management, resource use, data collection, and effective governance. Now that the contributors have addressed each, it's useful to take a look at how they complement one another, and what it takes to get started.

A New Way of Doing Business

Consider a scenario in which a state decides to adopt a Recovery School District model, of the kind discussed by Neerav Kingsland, for its failing schools. Implementing an RSD successfully takes more than just a bill from the state legislature and a declaration of intent from the state superintendent. Rather, a successful RSD requires new school models and a better use of data. One of the most important, if least commonly understood, functions of the leader of a Recovery School District is to serve as an ambassador for "a new way of doing business." As Kingsland adeptly explains, this is because an RSD must simultaneously work to expand the school marketplace, sup-port or close failing schools, and recruit new operators and human-capital providers to infuse the school system with the best educational options out there.

Relevant to this ambassador role is Michael Horn and Meg Evans's dis-cussion of how systems can cultivate a diverse array of schools so as to better meet diverse student needs. The challenge is that new providers do not just appear; instead, they must be identified, sought out, and, in some instances, convinced to invest in a new community. That's where the RSD ambassador comes in. When an RSD is collaborating with a team dedicated to supporting and facilitating new school development and delivery, it becomes a whole lot more likely that high-quality new schools will emerge. The same is true, of course, if the providers have access to the kind of professional practice and support that Doug Lemov envisions.

Access to accurate, detailed performance data and analysts with the skills and sophistication to make them useful are equally central to this work. With smart data management and analysis, ambassadors can identify school leaders or teachers with a track record of success, can help struggling schools identify high performers, can offer insights as to whether schools might be falling short in terms of instruction or operations, and can allow those cultivating and approving new schools to make informed decisions. Working in concert, data management and capable RSD leadership can successfully identify potential new school providers and leaders inside and outside of the system, then activate local and national networks to facilitate their recruitment.

Tackling Teacher Quality

Or consider the omnipresent challenge of teacher quality. While it's a leitmotif of contemporary school reform, any veteran superintendent or principal will tell you that improving quality is easier said than done. Moving beyond lip service requires an agenda that incorporates several moving pieces—addressing talent management, professional development, data, and resource use.

In gauging teacher quality and then using that information to drive decisions, Ranjit Nair explains the importance of both disciplined management and good data. Expanded data collection plays an equally prominent role when it comes to Doug Lemov's model of professional practice. Lemov notes that the data that have traditionally been collected for accountability purposes can, for instance, be used to identify successful teachers who can be more effectively leveraged to mentor less successful colleagues.

This professional practice requires meaningful data on teacher performance and competent analysts to study them. Jon Fullerton approaches data collection at a basic level: comprehensive collection and better management of data can improve teaching and guide decision-making. Yet, in many cases, efforts to improve data management overlook the needs that Lemov articulates. Creating opportunities for teachers to hone their practice is part and parcel of Ranjit Nair's comprehensive approach to human-capital management.

Lemov and Nair offer complementary strategies for attracting, cultivating, and retaining talented educators: first, they champion the development of formal mechanisms to recognize superior teachers through programs or events that highlight their achievements and give them nonfinancial compensation, praise, and respect. Second, they suggest ways to expand the career ladder for educators so that it no longer amounts to doing the same classroom work year after year or moving into an administrative role. Lemov proposes that districts develop teams of high-performing teachers to create resources like videos or model lesson plans to support broader district-wide teacher-training efforts. Such proposals offer educators the chance to take on new and interesting responsibilities without forcing them to leave the classroom.

Part and parcel of any conversation about improving the cultivation and management of talent is thinking on how to ensure that compensation more wisely acknowledges and rewards outstanding performance and outsized contributions. Here, the admonition of Karen Hawley Miles, Jonathan Travers, and Genevieve Green that employee salaries and benefits account for the largest share of school-system spending, and that this spending needs to support the larger mission, is an inescapable part of any sensible policy design.

Rebuilding the School District

Creating a diverse set of effective learning opportunities requires a shift in mindset, so that district leaders no longer presume that they must necessarily lead each and every local school—but embrace the notion that they might manage some schools and merely authorize, support, or monitor the presence of others. As Michael Horn and Meg Evans explain, the school system can serve as a "portfolio" manager that helps district and charter schools, online providers, private schools participating in voucher programs, and others serving students to peacefully coexist. Such an approach requires leaders to embrace Heather Zavadsky's observation that effective superintendents recognize the importance of accepting evolving definitions of system leadership.

A portfolio approach relies crucially upon a system of quality control that makes it possible to monitor school quality, encourage excellence, and address mediocrity. Michael Petrilli explains the challenges with finding the right balance for such a system, suggesting that authorities need to make distinctions between things that should be monitored based on inputs, like health and safety, and others that should not, like teacher and administrator certification.

PUTTING THE BLUEPRINT TO WORK

All of this amounts to an attempt to rethink the school district and its functions, so as to better meet the needs of twenty-first-century students—and take advantage of twenty-first-century tools. The contributors sketch a number of useful steps that state or local leaders can take in promoting systemic reform. Some suggestions require formal policy changes, while many require little more than the willingness of local officials, district leaders, or philanthropists to act boldly. Thus, the recommendations call for a broad coalition of actors at every level of the system.

State Legislators

Local leaders frequently benefit from the aid of state lawmakers. Contributors offer various suggestions that only state officials are in a position to address:

Alter funding systems to support advantageous external partnerships: State legislatures can use their budgeting power to strengthen the bargaining power of district officials when they negotiate with vendors. For example, access to high-speed Internet is now a basic classroom necessity, particularly in light of the expansion of online learning usage, but most schools have inadequate Internet infrastructures and limited access. In some areas, Internet providers have monopolized the marketplace, making service unduly expensive. Michael Horn and Meg Evans suggest that state legislatures use their budget authority to compel providers to come to the negotiating table with SEAs or districts.

They can do so by setting limits on Internet expenditures or offering tax breaks to companies that reduce fees for educational institutions. Additionally, state legislatures can create mechanisms through which to pay online providers based on student outcomes. Such contracts already exist in states like Florida and Utah; an online learning provider in Utah, for example, receives half of the funds up front and only receives the second half when a student completes a course.

Allocate funds to support better data systems: As Jon Fullerton notes, a robust, statewide data-management system is a cornerstone of any lasting school-improvement effort. State legislatures could allocate funds to support the development of such systems to replace those information systems, data warehouses, and analytical engines purchased individually by districts.

Fullerton explains that the type of rich data that teachers, principals, and school leaders need in order to understand what is working and what isn't requires more resources, capacity, and space than most districts can afford. Furthermore, current data collection taking place at the state and district level is a duplication of efforts, and consolidating data collection at the state-level could eventually reduce costs by eliminating this redundancy. A streamlined, centralized data warehouse would lay the groundwork for other reform efforts that rely on sophisticated data analysis like those outlined by Michael Petrilli, Doug Lemov, and Ranjit Nair.

Establish a Recovery School District: State legislatures are also empowered to enact policy changes. If there is public appetite and political will for an RSD, it is within the jurisdiction of the state legislature to sponsor a bill to establish one. This requires an individual or group of pioneering legislators to develop clear language, procedures, and rules for the authority of an RSD and specify how and when the RSD entity can intervene in district matters.

Any proposed legislation must also include explicit mechanisms for oversight to ensure that these rules are formally inserted into statewide accountability measures. Neerav Kingsland recommends that legislators sponsoring such a bill take "learning visits" to places where RSDs are successfully operating, such as Louisiana and Michigan, to better understand how and under what conditions an RSD can properly function, and then determine how to adapt it to their specific state context.

State Education Agencies

State education agencies (SEAs) have historically been low-profile organizations whose primary job was to manage. Today, of course, SEAs are increasingly acting as aggressive agents of system improvement. Some of the suggestions for SEAs include:

Improve the utility of school report cards: Michael Petrilli calls for state education agencies to support the improvement of school-level reports to make them universally comparable, easy-to-read, and more useful to families in school-choice-rich areas. Many of the existing school-level "report cards" across the country lack nonacademic information and showcase "student performance" numbers that come with little context. What's more, as Jon Fullerton notes, these report-card systems typically exclude private schools enrolling students via vouchers.

SEAs have greater capacity and more resources than individual districts to develop and maintain rich longitudinal data on all students and schools, including independent schools. Fullerton recommends ways to make report cards more parent-friendly, like offering descriptions of program offerings, instructional approaches, and the school community. SEAs could also consider outsourcing these reports to organizations such as GreatSchools (a national nonprofit that provides information on schools to parents) with proven track records of effectively communicating unbiased information about schools to the public.

Encourage local research consortia: Some large districts partner with local universities to share data and conduct joint research studies on critical issues in their classrooms, schools, and administrative offices. Fullerton describes the functions and benefits of such research consortia, referring to the well-established Consortium on Chicago School Research as well as newer efforts in New York, Michigan, Los Angeles, and Kansas City.

As Fullerton explains, a well-functioning research consortium acts as a thought partner for its agencies and the public, collecting and maintaining data over time, engaging stakeholders—like principals—in the selection of what to study, and interpreting research results. SEAs can encourage and support the creation of local research consortia by collecting and organizing data that districts can easily share with research partners and by brokering relationships between large districts—or a group of small districts—and universities.

Create a statewide teacher-screening process: Various contributors note the need to fundamentally rethink the ways teachers are identified, recruited, trained, evaluated, compensated, and employed. Drawing on existing models in high-achieving countries like Singapore and Finland, Ranjit Nair proposes that SEAs establish statewide pre-training teacher-selection systems that control admission into education programs and raise standards.

Whereas in some high-performing countries aspiring teachers must be in the top 20 or 30 percent of their graduating high school classes, many schools of education in the United States have some of the lowest admissions requirements of any degree programs. SEAs could leverage their regulatory and credentialing powers to mandate higher eligibility criteria for admission to education degree programs. If funds are available, SEAs could also attempt to attract high-achieving students to teacher-training programs by offering scholarships and grants.

Local Leaders

This whole effort proceeds from the presumption that many of the structures, policies, and practices designed for yesterday's schools and systems need to be rethought in the twenty-first century. Local leaders are responsible for driving much of this challenging work.

Redesign staffing and compensation models: Particularly in times of constrained finances, districts and school leaders can opt to explore new staffing designs and teacher-compensation models. Breaking away from traditional cost structures might entail, for example, maximizing students' exposure to the most talented teachers by increasing class sizes and paying those teachers more.

Jonathan Travers and his colleagues explain that such endeavors start with the superintendent carefully reviewing existing teacher-performance data and evaluating their workload. They also must understand the current distribution of effective teachers across schools and current teacher-compensation policies in order to propose changes to both. Such decisions require superintendents, principals, and human-resources staff to think differently about the role of a teacher, how to measure teacher effectiveness, and how to better utilize high-performing teachers. Leaders can't ignore the politics of such pursuits. As Heather Zavadsky notes, they must be prepared to defend these radical and likely controversial changes. On that score, she suggests they can learn from the experience of leaders in Baltimore, Charlotte, and Denver.

Allow school-level control over professional-development funds: Though district leaders are devolving decision-making authority to principals more and more, a number of centralized controls remain. As Doug Lemov points out, top-down mandates over the use of professional-development funds are vestiges of an outdated management approach that can be unnecessarily restrictive and unresponsive to school-level needs. Rather, he suggests that district leaders consider making professional-development funds more flexible at the school level. Lemov suggests that teacher development should grow out of individuals' experience in their school building and take into account school culture, structure, and practices, and thus encourages districts to decentralize professional-development funds so as to allow principals to create plans tailored to the needs and interests of the organization.

Negotiate performance-based contracts with external providers: Michael Horn and Meg Evans suggest that districts pursue performance-based contracts with online providers, textbook publishers, and other vendors as a way to ensure quality and control expenditures. For example, central offices or school boards could negotiate contracts directly with online vendors that stipulate the district will only pay part of the funds up front and hold the remainder in escrow until a student successfully completes a course or demonstrates competency on assessments.

Civic Actors

Contributors suggest that transformational change benefits from the cooperation of municipal agencies and civic leaders. For instance, useful steps worth considering include:

Create a mechanism to share teacher-performance data between schools: City support of shared data allows district, charter, and private schools to learn more, learn faster, and make smarter investments in talent management. In his chapter, Doug Lemov explains that the data that drive professional development respond to "network effects"; in other words, they offer greater insight when more people use them. Because school leaders benefit the more they can access data from other schools, it would be advantageous for this sharing practice to transcend the confines of a district.

The mayor and other city officials can step in here by developing a system that allows district, choice, and private schools to share teacher-performance data with each other. These data can help identify exemplary teachers whose pedagogical practices can be studied and shared among all schools in a city, for example. Information on what good teaching looks like can inform recruitment and selection efforts, like the state-level teacher-selection mechanism mentioned above.

Utilize local experts: Communities are filled with highly skilled professionals who are experts in areas, like human-capital management, that can be useful to school systems. Ranjit Nair suggests that local business executives nearing retirement could volunteer or be hired to advise district or school leaders on human-capital strategies that have proven successful in their industries.

One can imagine a scenario in which the local chamber of commerce hosts a convening of human-capital executives and human-resource officers from the district central office or surrounding schools. These business leaders might help school personnel think about designing an employee referral program to attract teacher candidates, work on retention plans for high-performing staff members, or help devise incentive schemes to motivate employees. They could serve as executive coaches and mentors for new principals and could leverage their professional networks to recruit additional volunteers to work in and support local schools.

Philanthropic support for a Recovery School District: Private foundation money has proven valuable in growing new school-reform efforts in a way that would be more difficult or slower to accomplish with public dollars alone. What's more, as Neerav Kingsland notes in his chapter, "local foundations often have significant influence over the political and business community." Using this influence, local philanthropists can position themselves to support entrepreneurial ventures, like an RSD.

In the case of an RSD, foundations can give money to help bring more high-performing charter-management organizations to the community to take over struggling schools, or expand facilities and staff for those already in place. They can also grant money to support promotion for the new district, like holding neighborhood school-choice fairs where families can learn about school options. Foundations can even use their influence to facilitate partnerships that improve RSD procedures and structure. For example, the Walton Family Foundation provided funds that allowed Louisiana's RSD to work with outside partners to design a central enrollment system, which eliminated many existing headaches in New Orleans.

A PATH FORWARD

The frustrating truth is that there are no permanent solutions in schooling, only solutions that make sense in a given place and time for the students being served. Yet, those charged with adjusting schools and systems to the exigencies of a new era are public officials who tend to prefer grand solutions that promise to avoid discomfort or disruption.

The resulting tension can readily yield a parody of swell-sounding reforms that amount to little. The result is that decades of feverish "reform" have done little to address the rigid and bureaucratic practices that have suffused management, staffing, compensation, and the educational enterprise for close to a century.

This volume offers a blueprint for tackling the perennial, seemingly intractable problems in today's education systems. It does so recognizing that transformational improvement will not occur within the confines of the existing institutional structures, policies, and practices. Instead, we present model examples of how to identify anachronistic and dysfunctional structures and policies that have impeded progress, and then construct ways to dismantle or entirely transform them. Approaching reform in this way opens up a wider landscape of possibility to create the schools and systems equal to the challenges of the twenty-first century.

Index

About the Contributors

Meg Evans is an education program associate at the Clayton Christensen Institute, where she runs the Institute's convening programs in education. She was previously an education research assistant at the Clayton Christensen Institute.

Jon Fullerton is the executive director of Harvard University's Center for Education Policy Research.

Genevieve Green is a principal associate at Education Resource Strategies, where she works with urban school districts on resource use and policy.

Frederick M. Hess is resident scholar and the director of Education Policy Studies at the American Enterprise Institute.

Taryn Hochleitner is a research associate in Education Policy Studies at the American Enterprise Institute.

Michael Horn is the cofounder and education executive director of the Clayton Christensen Institute, a nonprofit think tank that leverages the transformational power of disruptive innovation to solve society's most pressing problems. He is also the coauthor of *Disrupting Class: How Disruptive Innovation Will Change the Way the World Learns*.

Neerav Kingsland is chief executive officer of New Schools for New Orleans.

Doug Lemov is managing director of Uncommon Schools and author of *Teach Like a Champion.*

Karen Hawley Miles is president and executive director of Education Resource Strategies, a commissioner on the Equity and Excellence Commission for the U.S. Department of Education, and coauthor of *The Strategic School: Making the Most of People, Time and Money.*

Ranjit Nair is assistant professor at St. Edward's University and has over twenty years of experience leading human resources for multinational organizations. He is also the CEO of AlignThink, a management consultancy.

Michael J. Petrilli is executive vice president at the Thomas B. Fordham Institute, research fellow at Stanford University's Hoover Institution, and executive editor of Education Next.

Carolyn Sattin-Bajaj is assistant professor and codirector of the Center for College Readiness in the Department of Education Leadership, Management and Policy at Seton Hall University.

Jonathan Travers is a partner at Education Resource Strategies and leads the organization's district consulting practice.

Heather Zavadsky is the director of EdPractice Connect and author of *School Turnarounds: The Essential Role of Districts.*

Made in the USA
Middletown, DE
26 June 2019